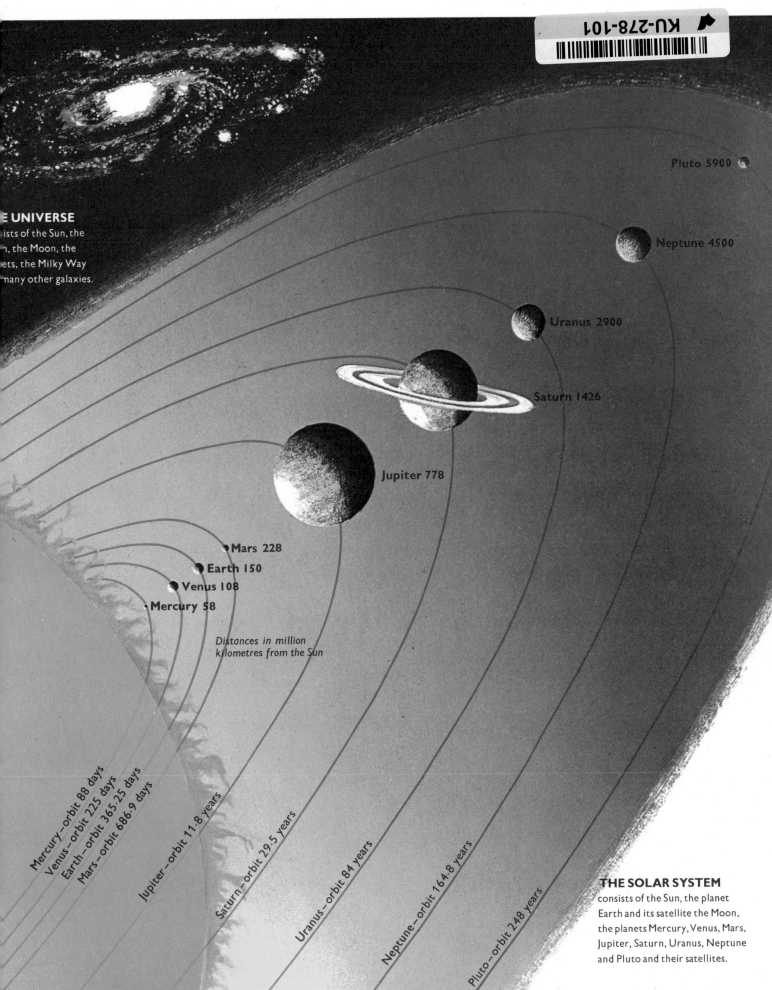

E UNIVERSE

...ists of the Sun, the
..., the Moon, the
...ets, the Milky Way
...many other galaxies.

Pluto 5900

Neptune 4500

Uranus 2900

Saturn 1426

Jupiter 778

Mars 228

Earth 150

Venus 108

Mercury 58

*Distances in million
kilometres from the Sun*

Mercury – orbit 88 days
Venus – orbit 225 days
Earth – orbit 365·25 days
Mars – orbit 686·9 days
Jupiter – orbit 11·8 years
Saturn – orbit 29·5 years
Uranus – orbit 84 years
Neptune – orbit 164·8 years
Pluto – orbit 248 years

THE SOLAR SYSTEM

consists of the Sun, the planet
Earth and its satellite the Moon,
the planets Mercury, Venus, Mars,
Jupiter, Saturn, Uranus, Neptune
and Pluto and their satellites.

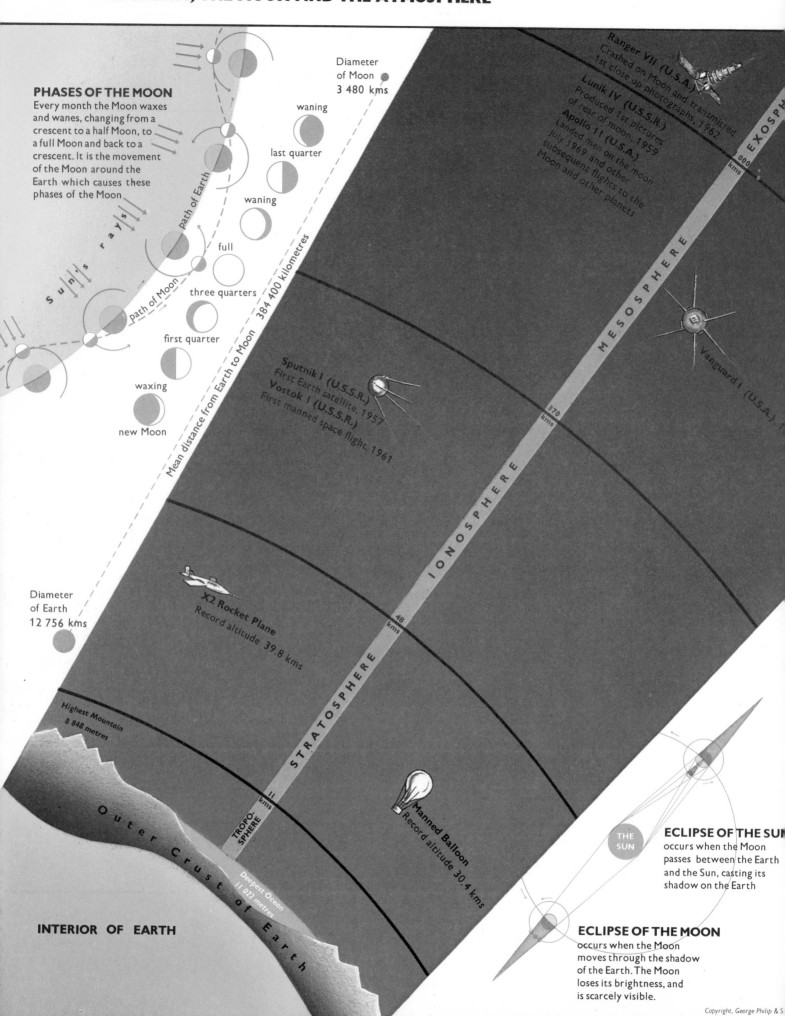

PHASES OF THE MOON

Every month the Moon waxes and wanes, changing from a crescent to a half Moon, to a full Moon and back to a crescent. It is the movement of the Moon around the Earth which causes these phases of the Moon

Sun's rays

path of Earth

path of Moon

waning

last quarter

waning

full

three quarters

first quarter

waxing

new Moon

Diameter of Moon
3 480 kms

Mean distance from Earth to Moon 384 400 kilometres

Diameter of Earth
12 756 kms

Ranger VII (U.S.A.)
Crashed on Moon and transmitted
1st close up photographs, 1962

Lunik IV (U.S.S.R.)
Produced 1st pictures
of rear of moon, 1959

Apollo 11 (U.S.A.)
Landed men on the moon
July 1969 and other
subsequent flights to the
Moon and other planets

EXOSPH

MESOSPHERE

IONOSPHERE

STRATOSPHERE

TROPO-SPHERE

1 000 kms

370 kms

48 kms

11 kms

Vanguard I (U.S.A.)

Sputnik I (U.S.S.R.)
First Earth satellite, 1957
Vostok I (U.S.S.R.)
First manned space flight, 1961

X2 Rocket Plane
Record altitude 39.8 kms

Highest Mountain
8 848 metres

Outer Crust of Earth

Deepest Ocean
11 022 metres

INTERIOR OF EARTH

Manned Balloon
Record altitude 30.4 kms

THE SUN

ECLIPSE OF THE SUN

occurs when the Moon passes between the Earth and the Sun, casting its shadow on the Earth

ECLIPSE OF THE MOON

occurs when the Moon moves through the shadow of the Earth. The Moon loses its brightness, and is scarcely visible.

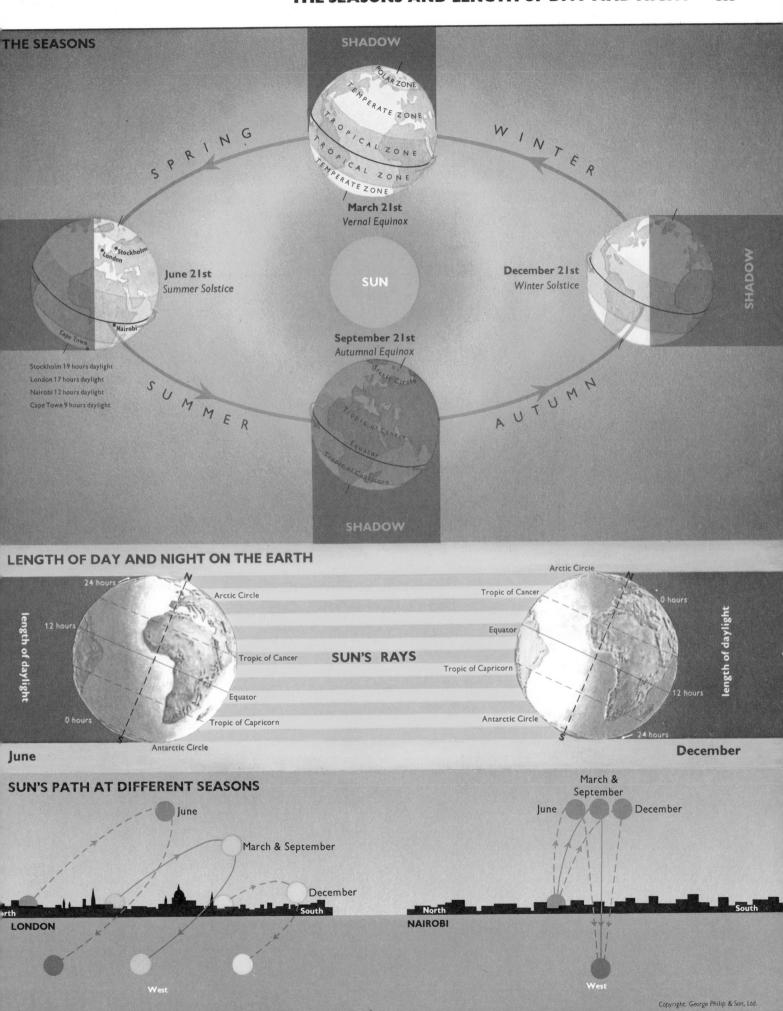

THE SEASONS

SPRING

WINTER

SHADOW

POLAR ZONE
TEMPERATE ZONE
TROPICAL ZONE
TROPICAL ZONE
TEMPERATE ZONE

March 21st
Vernal Equinox

Stockholm
London

June 21st
Summer Solstice

Nairobi

Cape Town

SUN

December 21st
Winter Solstice

SHADOW

Stockholm 19 hours daylight
London 17 hours daylight
Nairobi 12 hours daylight
Cape Town 9 hours daylight

SUMMER

September 21st
Autumnal Equinox

AUTUMN

Arctic Circle
Tropic of Cancer
Equator
Tropic of Capricorn

SHADOW

LENGTH OF DAY AND NIGHT ON THE EARTH

Arctic Circle

24 hours

12 hours

length of daylight

Arctic Circle

Tropic of Cancer

SUN'S RAYS

Tropic of Cancer

Equator

Tropic of Capricorn

0 hours

Equator

Tropic of Capricorn

Antarctic Circle

Antarctic Circle

0 hours

12 hours

length of daylight

24 hours

June

December

SUN'S PATH AT DIFFERENT SEASONS

June

March & September

December

North

South

LONDON

West

March & September

June

December

North

South

NAIROBI

West

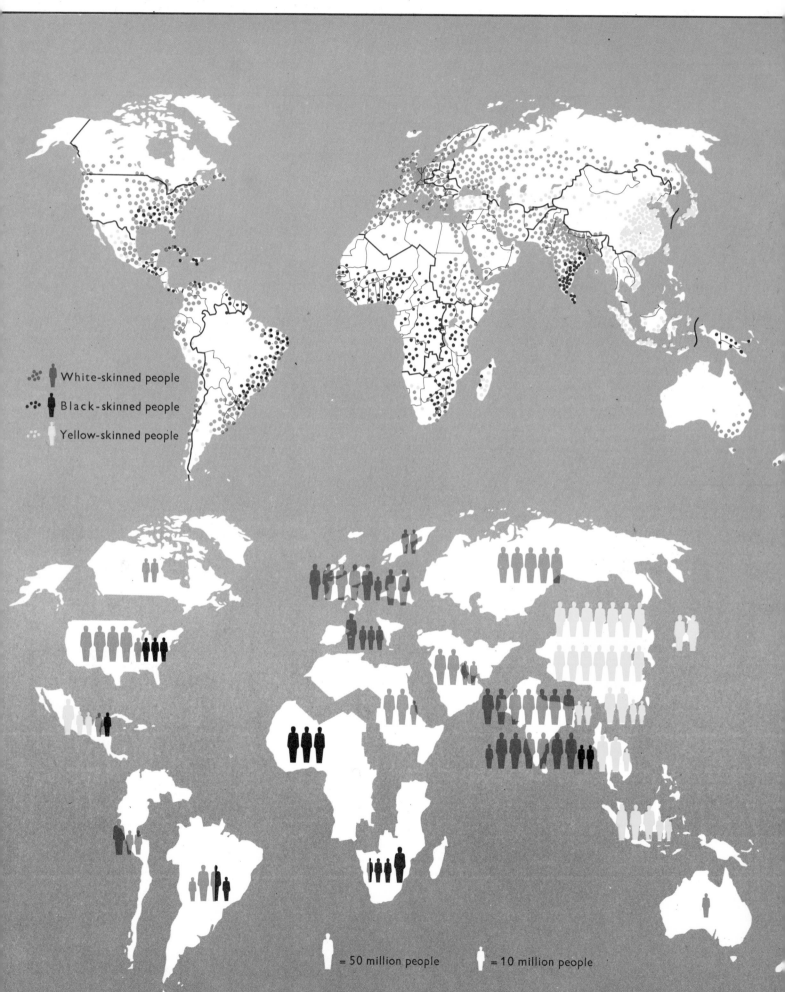

White-skinned people

Black-skinned people

Yellow-skinned people

= 50 million people   = 10 million people

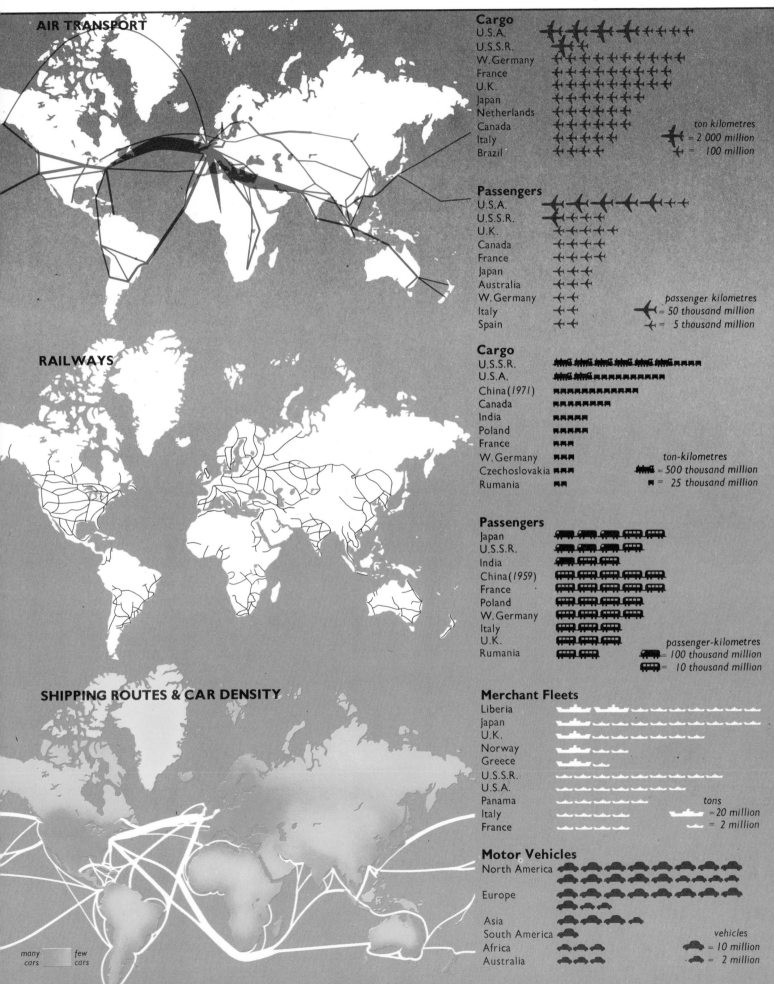

AIR TRANSPORT

Cargo
U.S.A.
U.S.S.R.
W. Germany
France
U.K.
Japan
Netherlands
Canada
Italy   = 2 000 million ton kilometres
Brazil   = 100 million

Passengers
U.S.A.
U.S.S.R.
U.K.
Canada
France
Japan
Australia
W. Germany   = 50 thousand million passenger kilometres
Italy
Spain   = 5 thousand million

RAILWAYS

Cargo
U.S.S.R.
U.S.A.
China (1971)
Canada
India
Poland
France
W. Germany
Czechoslovakia   = 500 thousand million ton-kilometres
Rumania   = 25 thousand million

Passengers
Japan
U.S.S.R.
India
China (1959)
France
Poland
W. Germany
Italy
U.K.   = 100 thousand million passenger-kilometres
Rumania   = 10 thousand million

SHIPPING ROUTES & CAR DENSITY

Merchant Fleets
Liberia
Japan
U.K.
Norway
Greece
U.S.S.R.
U.S.A.
Panama   = 20 million tons
Italy
France   = 2 million

Motor Vehicles
North America
Europe
Asia
South America   = 10 million vehicles
Africa
Australia   = 2 million

many cars   few cars

Copyright. George Philip & Son, Ltd.

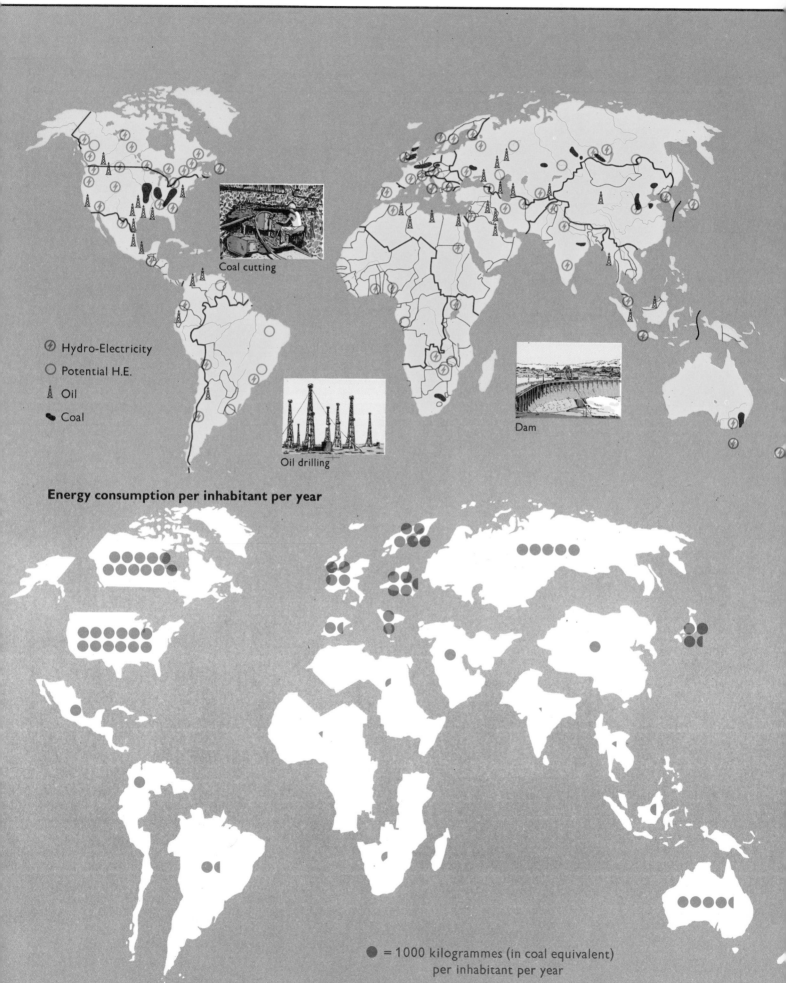

Hydro-Electricity
Potential H.E.
Oil
Coal

Coal cutting

Oil drilling

Dam

Energy consumption per inhabitant per year

● = 1000 kilogrammes (in coal equivalent)
per inhabitant per year

GENERAL REFERENCE

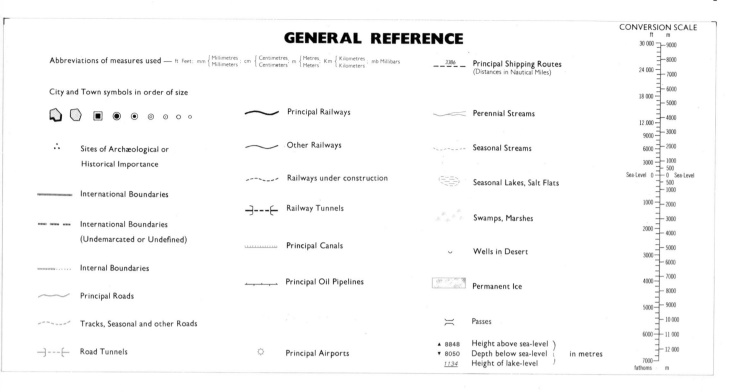

Abbreviations of measures used — ft Feet; mm {Millimetres / Millimeters} cm {Centimetres / Centimeters} m {Metres / Meters} Km {Kilometres / Kilometers} mb Millibars

City and Town symbols in order of size

∴ Sites of Archæological or Historical Importance

International Boundaries

International Boundaries (Undemarcated or Undefined)

Internal Boundaries

Principal Roads

Tracks, Seasonal and other Roads

Road Tunnels

Principal Railways

Other Railways

Railways under construction

Railway Tunnels

Principal Canals

Principal Oil Pipelines

☼ Principal Airports

Principal Shipping Routes (Distances in Nautical Miles)

Perennial Streams

Seasonal Streams

Seasonal Lakes, Salt Flats

Swamps, Marshes

Wells in Desert

Permanent Ice

Passes

▲ 8848 Height above sea-level
▼ 8050 Depth below sea-level } in metres
1134 Height of lake-level

CONVERSION SCALE

ft / m
30 000 — 9000
— 8000
24 000 — 7000
— 6000
18 000 — 5000
12.000 — 4000
9000 — 3000
3000 — 2000
— 1000
500
Sea-Level 0 — 0 Sea-Level
500
1000 — 1000
2000
2000 — 3000
4000
5000
3000 — 6000
7000
4000 — 8000
9000
5000 — 10 000
11 000
6000 — 12 000
7000
fathoms m

THE WORLD
Physical
1:150 000 000

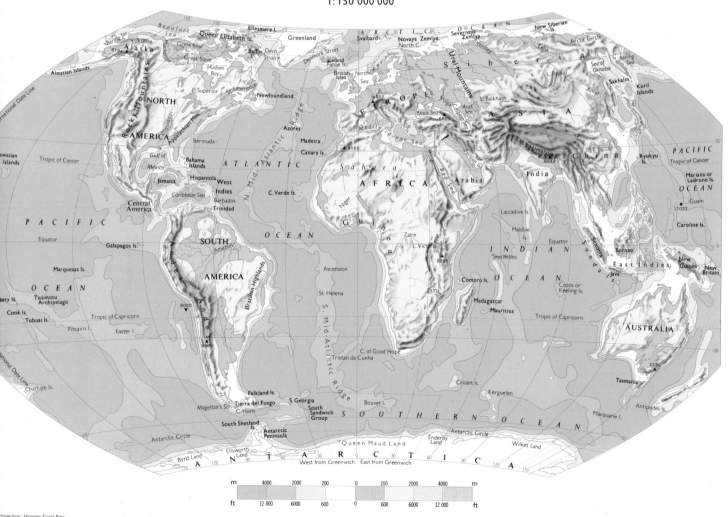

m 4000 2000 200 0 200 2000 4000 m
ft 12 000 6000 600 0 600 6000 12 000 ft

Projection: Hammer Equal Area

ARCTIC OCEAN

Novaya Zemlya
Franz Joseph Ld.
Severnaya Zemlya
Kotelny
New Siberian Is.
East Siberian Sea
Barents Sea
Kara Sea
Laptev Sea
Taymyr Pen.
Tiksi
Arctic Circle
Anadyr
Murmansk
Vorkuta
Verkhoyansk
Kolyma
Bering Sea

UNION OF SOVIET SOCIALIST REPUBLICS
Siberia
RUSSIAN SOVIET FEDERAL SOCIALIST REPUBLIC
Sea of Okhotsk
Kamchatka
Komandorskiye Is.
Petropavlovsk-Kamchatskiy
Rat Is.

Stockholm
Leningrad
Moskva
Gorkiy Kazan
Sverdlovsk
Novosibirsk
Tomsk Krasnoyarsk
Irkutsk
Ulan Ude
Chita
Blagoveshchensk
Komsomolsk
Khabarovsk
Sakhalin
C. Lopatka
Kuril Islands

Helsinki
Minsk
Warszawa
Kiyev
Kharkov
Donetsk
Rostov
Volgograd
Orenburg
Chelyabinsk
Omsk
Barnaul
Semipalatinsk
Hovd
Ulaanbaatar
MONGOLIA
Harbin
Changchun
Shenyang
Vladivostok
Sapporo
Hakodate

KAZAKHSTAN
Karaganda
L. Balkhash
Alma Ata
Wulumuchi
Peiping
Tientsin
Ta-tu
Sŏul
Pusan
JAPAN
Tōkyō
Yokohama
Nagoya
Ōsaka
Kōbe
Kyōto

Aral Sea
UZBEKISTAN
Tashkent
KIRGIZIA
Tarim
Soche (Yarkand)
CHINA
Lanchow
Sian
Tsinan
Tsingtao
Nanking
Shanghai
East China Sea

TURKEY
Tabriz
AFGHANISTAN
Kabul
Rawalpindi
KASHMIR
Srinagar
Indus
Tibet
Lhasa
Chengtu
Chungking
Wuhan
Changsha
PACIFIC OCEAN

LIBYA
EGYPT
SAUDI ARABIA
Nejd
Bahrain
QATAR
U.A.E.
OMAN
PAKISTAN
Karachi
INDIA
Delhi
Agra
Kanpur
Lucknow
Varanasi
NEPAL
BHUTAN
Brahmaputra
Dacca
Calcutta
BURMA
Kunming
Kwangchow
Hong Kong
TAIWAN
Taipei
Foochow

NIGER
CHAD
SUDAN
YEMEN
SOUTH YEMEN
G. of Aden
ETHIOPIA
SOMALI REP.
Arabian Sea
Bombay
Pune
Hyderabad
Nagpur
Bay of Bengal
Rangoon
THAILAND (SIAM)
Bangkok
CAMBODIA
VIET-NAM
Manila
PHILIPPINES
Quezon City
Cebu

Bangalore
Madras
Tiruchchirappalli
SRI LANKA (CEYLON)
Colombo
Andaman Is.
Nicobar Is.
Phnom Penh
G. of Siam
Saigon
South China Sea
Hainan

INDIAN OCEAN
Equator
Seychelles
Chagos Arch. (Br.)
Diego Garcia (Br.)
MALAYSIA
MALAYA
Kuala Lumpur
Singapore
Borneo
Sulawesi
Moluccas
Caroline Is. (U.S. Trust Territory)
Gilbert Is. (Br.)
Nauru

Maldive Is.
Sumatra
Palembang
INDONESIA
Jakarta
Bandung
Surabaya
Java
Irian Jaya
PAPUA NEW GUINEA
New Ireland
Admiralty Is.
Rabaul
New Britain
Solomon Is.
Tuvalu (Ellice Is.)

MADAGASCAR
Comoro Is.
Mozambique Chan.
Réunion (Fr.)
MAURITIUS
Cocos (Keeling) Is. (Australia)
Christmas I. (Australia)
Timor
Timor Sea
Arafura Sea
Torres Str.
C. York
Darwin
Port Moresby
Santa Cruz Is. (Br.)
Rotuma
New Hebrides (Br.-Fr.)
Fiji Is.
Viti Levu
Suva

ANGOLA
ZAMBIA
RHODESIA
BOTSWANA
SOUTH WEST AFRICA (NAMIBIA)
Tropic of Capricorn
NORTHERN TERRITORY
WESTERN AUSTRALIA
Alice Springs
Mt. Isa
Cairns
Townsville
QUEENSLAND
Rockhampton
Brisbane
New Caledonia
Nouméa
Norfolk I. (Australia)
Lord Howe I. (Australia)

SOUTH AFRICA
Johannesburg
Pretoria
Durban
Cape Town
C. of Good Hope
Port Elizabeth
Great Australian Bight
Perth
Fremantle
SOUTH AUSTRALIA
Adelaide
AUSTRALIA
NEW SOUTH WALES
Newcastle
Sydney
VICTORIA
Melbourne
TASMANIA
Hobart
Tasman Sea
NEW ZEALAND
Auckland
Wellington
Christchurch
Dunedin

SOUTHERN OCEAN
König Haakon VII Sea
Antarctic Circle
Enderby Land
Wilkes Land
Ross Sea
Magnetic Pole 1976

1:20 000 000

100   0   100   200   300   400   500 miles
100   0   200   400   600   800 km

CASPIAN SEA   -28

Ural   Ural Mountains   1617   Pechora   Ob   Obshchiye   Volga Uplands

Tundra   Kanin Peninsula   Mezen   Dvina   Volga   Don   Tsimlyansk Res.   Manych   Kuban   Terek   Kura   5165   Elbrus   5633

Kola Peninsula   White Sea   Onega   Onega   Ladoga   Rybinsk Res.   Oka   Volga   Central Russian Uplands   Sea of Azov   Crimea   5211   Caucasus   Rion   Araxes   Armenia   Kurdistan   Euphrates

Lapland   North Cape   Nordkinn   Finland   G. of Finland   Neva   Chudskoye   Valdai Hills   Pripyat   Pripyat Marshes   Dnepr (Dnieper)   Bug   Danube   BLACK SEA   Bosphorus   Anatolia   Taurus   3770   Cyprus   1951

Scandinavia   2123   Umeå   G. of Bothnia   Uleå   G. of Riga   Niemen   W. Dvina   Dniestr (Dniester)   Prut   Carpathians   2665   Transylvanian Alps   Wallachia   Balkans   Rhodope   Aegean Sea   Maritsa   Balkan Peninsula   Morea   5121   Matapan

Vesterålen   Lofoten   Gotland   BALTIC SEA   Vistula (Wisła)   North European Plain   Plain of Hungary   Tisza   Drava   Dinaric Alps   Pindus   Ionian Sea   Str. of Otranto

NORWEGIAN SEA   3734   Skagerrak   Kattegat   Jutland   Gotland   Öland   Mälaren   Vättern   Odra (Oder)   Elbe   Harz   1142   Erz Geb.   Sudetes   Moravia   Bohemian For.   Danube   ADRIATIC SEA   Sasso   Apennines   Vesuvius   1277   Etna   3263   Sicily   MEDITERRANEAN SEA

Arctic Circle   Iceland   Hvannadalshnúkur 2119   Faroe Is.   FAEROES   Shetland Is.   Fair Isle   Orkney Is.   North Sea   FISHER   VIKING   GERMAN BIGHT   Heligoland   Netherlands   Wesel   Weser   Rhine   Black For.   Vosges   Taunus   Alps   Po   Ligurian Sea   Corsica   Str. of Bonifacio   Sardinia   C. Blanco   Tyrrhenian Sea   Str. of Messina   Calabria   Malta

ATLANTIC OCEAN   Rockall Bank   FORTIES   DOGGER   Dogger Bank   HUMBER   THAMES   DOVER   Great Britain   English Channel   Brittany   Loire   Seine   Central Massif 1886   Cévennes   G. of Lions   Maritime Alps   Plateau of the Shotts   Atlas   Saharan Atlas

Fisher Bank   Hebrides   Ben Nevis 1344   British Isles   Snowdon 1085   Ireland   Irish Sea   Land's End   C. Clear   Valentia   SHANNON   FASTNET   LUNDY   Bay of Biscay   Gironde   Garonne   Pyrenees 3404   Iberian Peninsula   New Castile   Old Castile   Cantabrian Mts.   Sierra Morena   Guadalquivir   Sierra Nevada 3478   Andalusia   Str. of Gibraltar

Projection: Bonne   West from Greenwich 0 East from Greenwich

ft   m   4000   2000   1000   600   200   0   200   600   2000   4000   ft   m
12 000   6000   3000   1200   600   0   600   6000   12 000

1 : 4 000 000

20   0   20   40   60 miles
10   0   20   40   60   80 km

The DISTRICTS of Northern Ireland have been numbered and can be identified by reference to this table.

1	Londonderry	14	Craigavon
2	Limavady	15	Armagh
3	Coleraine	16	Newry & Mourne
4	Ballymoney	17	Banbridge
5	Moyle	18	Down
6	Larne	19	Lisburn
7	Ballymena	20	Antrim
8	Magherafelt	21	Newtownabbey
9	Cookstown	22	Carrickfergus
10	Strabane	23	North Down
11	Omagh	24	Ards
12	Fermanagh	25	Castlereagh
13	Dungannon	26	Belfast

1 Merseyside
2 Greater Manchester
3 West Yorkshire
4 South Yorkshire
5 West Glamorgan
6 Mid Glamorgan
7 South Glamorgan

Orkney Is.

Shetland Is.

Projection : Conical with two standard parallels

West from Greenwich   East from Greenwich

COPYRIGHT. GEORGE PHILIP & SON. LTD.

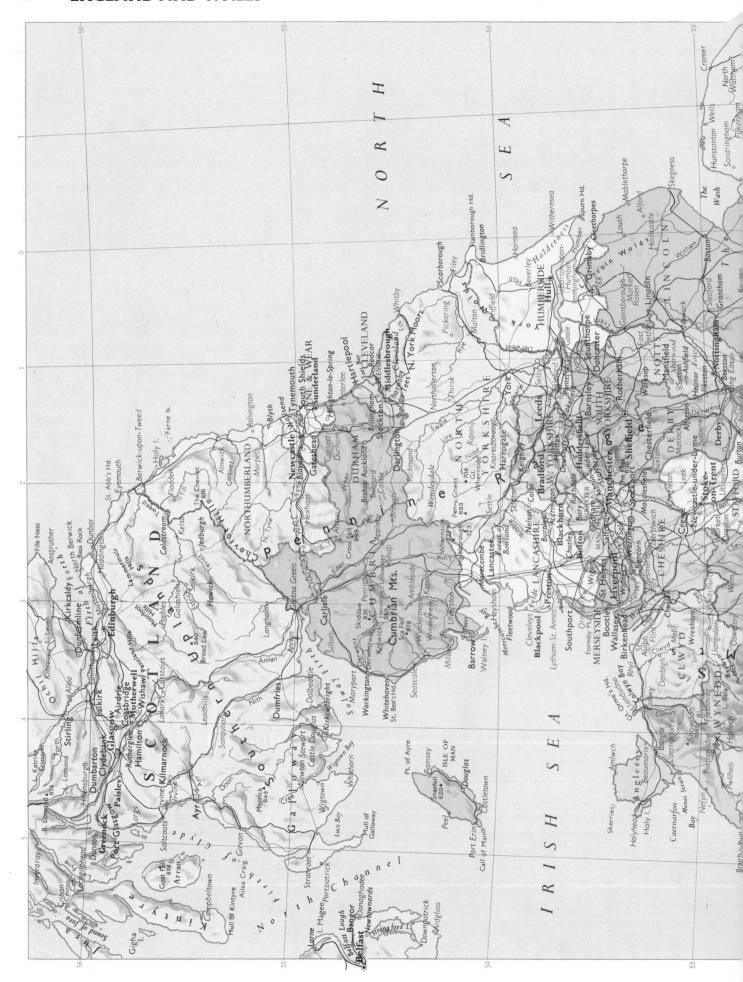

1 : 2 000 000

```
10        0        10        20        30        40   50 miles
10   0   10   20   30   40   50   60   70   80 km
```

SCILLY ISLES
On same Scale

St. Ives
Penzance
Land's End
Isles of Scilly
St. Mary's

ENGLISH CHANNEL

FRANCE

East from Greenwich

West from Greenwich

Projection : Conical with two standard parallels.

COPYRIGHT GEORGE PHILIP & SON LTD.

Major place names and regions shown on the map include:

Southwold, Aldeburgh, Orford Ness, Felixstowe, Harwich, Ipswich, SUFFOLK, Clacton, Southend, Colchester, ESSEX, Chelmsford, Margate, Ramsgate, Deal, Dover, Folkestone, Canterbury, Hythe, New Romney, Dungeness, Hastings, Eastbourne, Beachy Hd., KENT, Maidstone, Rochester, Chatham, Gillingham, Gravesend, Ashford, Tunbridge Wells, EAST SUSSEX, Brighton, Worthing, Newhaven, Hove, WEST SUSSEX, Chichester, Bognor Regis, Littlehampton, Selsey Bill, Hayling I., Portsmouth, Gosport, Ryde, ISLE OF WIGHT, Newport, Cowes, Ventnor, St. Catherine's Point, The Needles, Southampton, Winchester, Eastleigh, Fareham, HANTS, Salisbury, WILTS, Stonehenge, Swindon, BERKS, Reading, Newbury, Andover, SURREY, Guildford, Croydon, LONDON, Harrow, Ealing, Barnet, Enfield, Watford, HERTFORD, St. Albans, Luton, BEDFORD, Bedford, Northampton, NORTHAMPTON, CAMBRIDGE, Cambridge, BUCKS, OXFORD, Oxford, Aylesbury, High Wycombe, Maidenhead, Windsor, Slough, Thames, Cotswold Hills, Cheltenham, GLOUCESTER, Gloucester, Stroud, Cirencester, Swindon, Bristol, AVON, Bath, Trowbridge, Frome, Mendip Hills, Weston-super-Mare, Bridgwater, SOMERSET, Taunton, Wellington, Yeovil, DORSET, Dorchester, Weymouth, Portland Bill, Poole, Bournemouth, Christchurch, Blandford, Sherborne, Bridport, Lyme Regis, Axminster, Honiton, Exmouth, Teignmouth, Torquay, TORBAY, Paignton, DEVON, Exeter, Tiverton, Barnstaple, Ilfracombe, Minehead, Exmoor, Dartmoor, Okehampton, Tavistock, Plymouth, Devonport, Salcombe, Kingsbridge, Start Pt., Dartmouth, Totnes, Newton Abbot, Bideford, Bude, Boscastle, Newquay, CORNWALL, Bodmin, Bodmin Moor, Brown Willy, Launceston, St. Austell, Fowey, Looe, Truro, Redruth, Camborne, Helston, Falmouth, Lizard, Penzance, St. Ives, St. Michael's Mount, Land's End

WALES: POWYS, GWENT, Cardiff, Newport, Swansea, Rhondda, MID GLAMORGAN, SOUTH GLAMORGAN, WEST GLAMORGAN, Merthyr Tydfil, Aberdare, Pontypridd, Bridgend, Port Talbot, Neath, Brecon Beacons, Black Mts., DYFED, Carmarthen, Llanelli, Tenby, Pembroke, Milford Haven, Haverfordwest, St. David's Hd., Fishguard, Cardigan, Aberystwyth, Cardigan Bay, Newtown, HEREFORD & WORCESTER, Hereford, Worcester, Malvern Hills, Kidderminster, Ludlow, Bridgnorth, WARWICK, Birmingham, Coventry, Leamington, WEST MIDLANDS, Dudley, Stourbridge, Redditch, Stratford-on-Avon, Banbury

FRANCE: Dieppe, Rouen, Le Havre, Cherbourg, Caen, Bayeux, Lisieux, Bernay, Honfleur, Trouville, Fécamp, Étretat, Yvetot, St. Valéry, Le Tréport, Pont l'Évêque, Elbeuf, Louviers, C. de la Hague, C. de la Hève, Barfleur, Valognes, Carentan, Périers, Isigny, Arromanches, Vierville, St. Lô, Alderney, Sark, St. Peter Port, Guernsey, Jersey, St. Helier, Channel Islands

Bristol Channel, Lundy, Hartland Point

1 : 2 000 000

10   0   10   20   30   40   50 miles
10   0   10   20   30   40   50   60   70   80 km

ORKNEY IS.
On same scale

Scapa Flow
Hoy
South Ronaldsay
North Ronaldsay
Westray
Rousay
Eday
Sanday
Stronsay
Stromness
Mainland
Shapinsay
ORKNEY
Kirkwall
Scapa Flow
Hoy
South Ronaldsay
Pentland Firth
Dunnet Hd.
John O'Groats

SHETLAND IS.
On same scale

Unst
Yell
Fetlar
Yell Sound
SHETLAND
Whalsay
Mainland
Bressay
Foula
Scalloway
Lerwick
Sumburgh Hd.

Map labels

Butt of Lewis
Flannan Is.
L. Roag
Broad Bay
Stornoway
Lewis
Eye Pen.
WESTERN ISLES
Outer Hebrides
Tarbert
Harris
L. Seaforth
Sound of Harris
North Uist
Lochmaddy
Monach Is.
Benbecula
South Uist
Ben More
Lochboisdale
Barra
Sound of Barra
Barra Hd.

C. Wrath
Durness
Strathy Pt.
Orkney Is.
Pentland Firth
Dunnet Hd.
Thurso
John O'Groats
Noss Hd.
Wick
Lybster
L. Laxford
Eddrachillis Bay
L. Assynt
B. More Assynt
Reay Forest
Ben Hope 927
Tongue
Halladale
L. Loyal
Naver
Loch Shin
Lairg
Brora
Brora
Golspie
Ord of Caithness
Helmsdale
Helmsdale
Enard Bay
Lochinver
Ullapool
L. Broom
Oykell
Dornoch
Dornoch Firth
Tain
Tarbat Ness
Moray Firth
Lossiemouth
Cullen
Portsoy
Banff Macduff
Buckie
Kinnaird's Head
Fraserburgh
Rattray Head
Peterhead
Buchan Ness
The Aird
L. Gairloch
Trotternish
Rona
L. Maree
L. Fannich
B. Dearg 1081
Strathpeffer
Invergordon
Ben Wyvis 1045
Cromarty
Conon
Dingwall
Elgin
Forres
Rothes
Keith
Deveron
Turriff
Elton
Ythan
BUCHAN
WEST HIGHLANDS
NORTH HIGHLANDS
HIGHLAND
Portree
Sound of Raasay
Raasay
L. Torridon
Glen Affric
Beauly
Inverness
Culloden Moor
Nairn
Findhorn
GRAMPIAN
Inverurie
Huntly
Alford
Don
Dufftown
Skye
Cuillin Hills
Kyle of Lochalsh
Dornie
Stromeferry
Carron
Glen Moriston
Fort Augustus
Loch Ness
Glen Garry
Grantown-on-Spey
Strath Spey
Aviemore
Monadhliath Mts.
Kingussie
Cairn Gorm 1245
Cairngorm Mts.
Cairn Toul 1292
Ben Macdhui 1311
Ballater
Aboyne
Balmoral
Banchory
Aberdeen
Girdle Ness
Cuillin Sound
Canna
Rhum
Eigg
Muck
L. Moidart
Mallaig
L. Morar
Arisaig
L. Eil
Ben Nevis 1343
Fort William
Loch Arkaig
L. Oich
Newtonmore
Badenoch
Forest of Atholl
Lochnagar 1154
Braemar
N. Esk
Braes of Angus
Laurencekirk
Inverbervie
Stonehaven
Ardnamurchan Pt.
Coll
Loch Sunart
Ardgour
Morvern
Glen Coe
Ballachulish
Rannoch Moor
Garry
Blair Atholl
Pass of Killiecrankie
Pitlochry
Kirriemuir
S. Esk
Brechin
Montrose
Tiree
Tobermory
Staffa
Mull
Ben More 966
Iona
Firth of Lorn
Lismore
Loch Linnhe
Loch Etive
Ben Cruachan 1124
Ben Lawers 1214
L. Tay
Breadalbane
Aberfeldy
Dunkeld
Tay
Blairgowrie
Alyth
Isla
Forfar
Sidlaw Hills
Arbroath
Broughty Ferry
Dundee
TAYSIDE
Oban
Ben More 1174
B. Vorlich 983
Crieff
Earn
Comrie
Perth
Scone
Carse of Gowrie
Firth of Tay
Tayport
St. Andrews
Fife Ness
Anstruther
FIFE
Cupar
Leven
Colonsay
Rubh' a' Mhail
Loch Awe
B. Vorlich 942
Inveraray
Lomond
Loch Katrine
Trossachs
Ben Lomond 974
Callander
CENTRAL
Dunblane
Stirling
Bannockburn
Ochil Hills
Kinross
L. Leven
Loch Lomond
Glenrothes
Lochgelly
Buckhaven
Kirkcaldy
Dunfermline
Alloa
Cowdenbeath
Crinan
Jura
Sound of Jura
Lochgilphead
Heleensburgh
Dumbarton
Clydebank
Glasgow
Grangemouth
Linlithgow
Falkirk
Rosyth
Leith
Edinburgh
LOTHIAN
Haddington
North Berwick
Dunbar
Bass Rock
Firth of Forth
St. Abbs Hd.
Eyemouth
Loch Fyne
Dunoon
Greenock
Port Glasgow
Paisley
Renfrew
Rutherglen
Airdrie
Coatbridge
Motherwell
Wishaw
Hamilton
Kilbride
Kirkintilloch
Bathgate
Penicuik
Dalkeith
Musselburgh
Pentland Hills
Moorfoot Hills
Lammermuir Hills
Duns
Coldstream
Berwick on Tweed
Holy I.
Islay
Bowmore
Port Ellen
Gigha
Largs
Rothesay
Bute
Ardrossan
Saltcoats
Troon
Prestwick
Ayr
Kilmarnock
Irvine
Kilmaunock
Carstairs
Lanark
Biggar
Peebles
Tweed
Galashiels
Selkirk
Melrose
Kelso
Flodden
Till
The Cheviot 816
STRATHCLYDE
Goat Fell 874
Arran
Brodick
Campbeltown
Kintyre
Mull of Kintyre
Ailsa Craig
Girvan
Doon
Dalmellington
Cumnock
Leadhills
Sanquhar
Nith
Moffat
Broad Law 840
Ettrick
Teviot
Hawick
Jedburgh
Cheviot Hills
N. Tyne
Coquet
BORDERS
Southern Uplands
SOUTHERN UPLANDS
Merrick 843
Ken
Newton Stewart
Castle Douglas
Dalbeattie
DUMFRIES AND GALLOWAY
Dumfries
Annan
Lockerbie
Gretna Green
Langholm
Esk
Liddel
ENGLAND
Hexham
Carlisle
HADRIAN'S WALL
Tyne
Alston
Wear
Cross Fell 893
Tees
Barnard Castle
Workington
Penrith
Ullswater
Skiddaw 931
Derwent
Cumbrian Mts.
NORTH SEA
ATLANTIC OCEAN
North Minch
Inner Hebrides
Little Minch
Sound of Sleat
Loch Linnhe
Firth of Clyde
North Channel
Solway Firth
Wigtown Bay
Luce Bay
Mull of Galloway
Galloway
Newton Stewart
Wigtown
Whithorn
Stranraer
Portpatrick
L. Ryan
Rathlin
Fair Hd.
Mull of Kintyre
Ballycastle
Trostan 554
NORTHERN IRELAND
Ballymena
Larne
Belfast Lough
Belfast
Bangor
Newtownards

Projection : Conical with two standard parallels.

West from Greenwich

1 : 2 000 000

10 0 10 20 30 40 50 miles
10 0 10 20 30 40 50 60 70 80 km

Legend

Towns underlined in Northern Ireland give their names to the Districts in which they stand

The remaining Districts are:—

1	Fermanagh	5	Castlereagh
2	Moyle	6	Ards
3	Newtownabbey	7	Down
4	North Down	8	Newry & Mourne

Projection: Conical with two standard parallels.

West from Greenwich

COPYRIGHT. GEORGE PHILIP & SON. LTD.

Oceans and Seas

ATLANTIC OCEAN

North Channel

IRISH SEA

St. George's Channel

Provinces

ULSTER · CONNACHT · LEINSTER · MUNSTER

NORTHERN IRELAND

IRELAND

Counties and Regions

DONEGAL · LONDONDERRY · ANTRIM · TYRONE · FERMANAGH · MONAGHAN · CAVAN · LEITRIM · SLIGO · MAYO · ROSCOMMON · LONGFORD · WESTMEATH · MEATH · LOUTH · DUBLIN · KILDARE · OFFALY · LAOIS · GALWAY · CLARE · LIMERICK · TIPPERARY · KILKENNY · CARLOW · WICKLOW · WEXFORD · WATERFORD · CORK · KERRY

Selected places

Kintyre · Arran · Campbeltown · Mull of Kintyre · Ailsa Craig · Stranraer · Portpatrick

Malin Hd. · Tory I. · Horn Hd. · Sheep Haven · Lough Swilly · Carndonagh · Inishowen Pen. · Moville · Buncrana · Rathlin I. · Giant's Causeway · Portrush · Ballycastle · Fair Hd. · Bloody Foreland · Gweedore · Errigal 752 · Derryveagh Mts. · Letterkenny · Coleraine · Limavady · Ballymoney · Mt. Trostan 554 · Larne

Londonderry · Strabane · Sperrin Mts. · Sawel 683 · Magherafelt · Ballymena · Antrim · Carrickfergus · Belfast L. · Belfast · Bangor · Donaghadee · Ards Pen. · Newtownards · Lisburn · Strangford L.

Gweebarra B. · Glenties · Bluestack 676 · Finn · Lifford · Cookstown · Omagh · Dungannon · Portadown · Lurgan (Craigavon) · Armagh · Banbridge · Downpatrick · Dundrum

Rossan Pt. · Rathlin O Birne I. · Killybegs · Donegal · Ballyshannon · Bundoran · Enniskillen · L. Erne · Irvinestown · Blackwater · Newry · Sl. Gullion 577 · Mourne Mts. · Slieve Donard 852 · Newcastle · Warrenpoint · Dundrum Bay

Donegal Bay · Sligo B. · Sligo · Collooney · L. Allen · Leitrim · Belturbet · Annalee · Clones · Upper L. Erne · Cootehill · Cavan · Carrickmacross · Castleblayney · Monaghan · Carling ford L. · Greenore · Dundalk · Dundalk Bay

Broad Haven · Erris Hd. · Belmullet · Mullet Peninsula · Killala · Ballina · Killala B. · Ox Mts. · Boyle · Carrick-on-Shannon · Kingscourt · Ardee · Louth

Achill Hd. · Achill I. · Clare I. · Nephin 806 · L. Conn · Castlebar · Castlereagh · L. Arrow · Gowna · Granard · Longford · Kingscourt · Ceanannas Mor (Kells) · Blackwater · Olocastle · L. Sheelin · Drogheda · Balbriggan

Clew Bay · Croagh Patrick 765 · Westport · Robe · Claremorris · Roscommon · L. Ree · Athboy · An Uaimh (Navan) · Trim · Boyne · Swords · Lambay I.

Killary Harbour · Mweelrea 819 · Inishbofin · L. Mask · Ballinrobe · Tuam · Suck · Mullingar · Maynooth · Dublin · Ireland's Eye · Howth Head

Twelve Pins · Clifden · Slyne Hd. · Connemara · L. Corrib · L. Corrib · Athlone · WESTMEATH · Clara · Edenderry · Celbridge · Dublin (Baile Átha Cliath) · Dublin Bay · Dun Laoghaire

Kilkieran B. · Galway · Athenry · Loughrea · Ballinasloe · Clare · Tullamore · Daingean · Droichead Nua · Naas · Bray

Galway Bay · Inishmore · Aran Is. · Gort · Slieve Aughty · Portumna · Shannon · Birr · Sl. Bloom · Portarlington · Mountmellick · Port Laoise · Kildare · Kippure 754 · Poulaphouca Res.

Hags Hd. · Liscannor · Liscannor Bay · Ennistymon · L. Derg · Roscrea · Athy · Barrow · LEINSTER · Wicklow · Wicklow Hd.

Mal Bay · Miltown Malbay · Ennis · Killaloe · Ballina · Nenagh · Templemore · Carlow · Tullow · Shillelagh · Gorey · Arklow · Lugnaquillia 923 · Mizen Hd.

Kilkee · Kilrush · Loop Hd. · Rineanna · Ardnacrusha · Keeper 694 · Thurles · Slievenamon 722 · Kilkenny · Muine Bheag · Mt. Leinster 796 · Cahore Pt.

R. Shannon · Foynes · Rathkeale · Limerick · TIPPERARY · Cashel · Callan · Enniscorthy · WEXFORD

Kerry Hd. · Tralee Bay · Listowel · Newcastle · Rath Luirc (Charleville) · Tipperary · Caher · Clonmel · Carrick-on-Suir · New Ross · Wexford · Wexford Harbour · Rosslare · Greenore Pt. · Tuscar Rock

Brandon Bay · Brandon Mt. 953 · Dingle · Sl. Mish · Maine · Newmarket · Mitchelstown · Knockmealdown Mts. · Comeragh Mts. · Waterford · Tramore · Carnsore Pt.

Gt. Blasket I. · Dunmore Hd. · Dingle Bay · Killarney · Kanturk · Mallow · Fermoy · Blackwater · Lismore · Dungarvan · Dungarvan Bay · Hook Hd. · Waterford Harbour · Saltee Is.

Valentia Harbour · Valentia I. · Cahirciveen · Macgillycuddy Reeks · Carrantuohill 1040 · Lakes of Killarney · Boggeragh Mts. · Macroom · Blarney · Cork · Youghal · Youghal Harbour · St. David's Hd.

Skellig Rocks · Kenmare · Caha Mts. · Glengarriff · Lee · Midleton · Cobh · Cork Harbour · Passage West · Crosshaven · Kinsale

Ballinskelligs B. · Castletown Bearhaven · Bantry · Bandon · Clonakilty · Skibbereen · Old Head of Kinsale

Bear I. · Bantry Bay · Crow Hd. · Skull · Clonakilty Bay · Galley Hd. · Fastnet Rock

Dunmanus Bay · Mizen Hd. · Baltimore · C. Clear · Clear I.

East from Greenwich

1:5 000 000

20 10 0 20 40 60 80 100 miles
40 20 0 40 80 120 160 km

FRENCH DEPARTMENTS

Abbr.	No.	Department
Ai.	01	Ain
Ai.	02	Aisne
Al.	03	Allier
A.H.P.	04	Alpes-de-Haute-Provence
H.A.	05	Hautes-Alpes
A.M.	06	Alpes-Maritimes
Ard.	07	Ardèche
Ard.	08	Ardennes
Ari.	09	Ariège
Au.	10	Aube
Au.	11	Aude
Av.	12	Aveyron
B.R.	13	Bouches-du-Rhône
C.	14	Calvados
Ca.	15	Cantal
Ch.	16	Charente
Ch.M.	17	Charente-Maritime
Che.	18	Cher
Co.	19	Corrèze
C.O.	20	Corse a) Haute-Corse b) Corse-du-Sud
C.O.	21	Côte-d'Or
C.N.	22	Côtes-du-Nord
Cr.	23	Creuse
D.	24	Dordogne
Do.	25	Doubs
Dr.	26	Drôme
E.	27	Eure
E.L.	28	Eure-et-Loir
F.	29	Finistère
G.	30	Gard
H.G.	31	Haute-Garonne
Ge.	32	Gers
Gi.	33	Gironde
H.	34	Hérault
I.V.	35	Ille-et-Vilaine
I.	36	Indre
I.L.	37	Indre-et-Loire
Is.	38	Isère
J.	39	Jura
L.	40	Landes
L.C.	41	Loir-et-Cher
Loi.	42	Loire
H.L.	43	Haute-Loire
L.A.	44	Loire-Atlantique
Loi.	45	Loiret
Lo.	46	Lot
L.G.	47	Lot-et-Garonne
Loz.	48	Lozère
M.L.	49	Maine-et-Loire
Ma.	50	Manche
Ma.	51	Marne
H.M.	52	Haute-Marne
May.	53	Mayenne
M.M.	54	Meurthe-et-Moselle
Me.	55	Meuse
Mo.	56	Morbihan
Mos.	57	Moselle
N.	58	Nièvre
No.	59	Nord
O.	60	Oise
Or.	61	Orne
P.C.	62	Pas-de-Calais
P.D.	63	Puy-de-Dôme
P.A.	64	Pyrénées Atlantiques
H.P.	65	Hautes Pyrénées
P.O.	66	Pyrénées (Orientales)
B.R.	67	Bas Rhin
H.R.	68	Haut Rhin
Rh.	69	Rhône
H.S.	70	Haute Saône
S.L.	71	Saône-et-Loire
Sa.	72	Sarthe
H.S.	73	Haute-Savoie
Sa.	74	Savoie
S.Me.	75	Paris
S.Me.	76	Seine-Maritime
S.M.	77	Seine-et-Marne
Y.	78	Yvelines
D.S.	79	Deux-Sèvres
So.	80	Somme
T.	81	Tarn
T.G.	82	Tarn-et-Garonne
Va.	83	Var
Va.	84	Vaucluse
Ve.	85	Vendée
Vi.	86	Vienne
H.V.	87	Haute Vienne
Vo.	88	Vosges
Y.	89	Yonne
B.	90	Belfort
Es.	91	Essonne
H.S.	92	Hauts-de-Seine
S.S.D.	93	Seine-St-Denis
V.M.	94	Val-de-Marne
V.O.	95	Val-d'Oise

CORSICA
On same scale

Corse • Bastia
Calvi • Haute-Corse
Mt. Cinto 2710 • Pta. Rotondo 2625
Corse du Sud
Ajaccio • Porto Vecchio
Bonifacio

Projection: Conical with two standard parallels

East from Greenwich · West from Greenwich

1:5 000 000

50   0   50   100 miles

50   0   50   100   150 km

East from Greenwich

West from Greenwich

Projection: Conical with two standard parallels

FRANCE

SPAIN

PORTUGAL

ALGERIA

MOROCCO

Madrid · Barcelona · Valencia · Zaragoza · Sevilla · Málaga · Bilbao · Lisboa · Porto · Toulouse · Perpignan · Gerona · Palma · Mallorca · Menorca · Ibiza · Cabrera · Formentera

Pyrénées · Andorra · Navarra · Aragón · Castilla La Vieja · Castilla La Nueva · Extremadura · Galicia · Asturias · Cantábrica · Cordillera Cantábrica · Sierra de Guadarrama · Sierra de Gredos · Sierra Morena · Sierra Nevada · Serranía de Cuenca · Sierra de Albarracín · Montes de Toledo · La Mancha

Alger · Thenia · Bouffarik · Koléa · Blida · Khemis · Miliana · El Asnam · Mostaganem · Oran · Mohammadia · Sig · Tanger · Tetouan · Ceuta · Gibraltar

Bay of Biscay · ATLANTIC OCEAN · MEDITERRANEAN SEA · Islas Baleares · Golfo de Valencia · Golfo de San Jorge · Golfo de Cádiz · Strait of Gibraltar

La Coruña · Santiago de Compostela · Vigo · Pontevedra · Orense · Lugo · Oviedo · Gijón · León · Burgos · Palencia · Valladolid · Zamora · Salamanca · Ávila · Segovia · Cáceres · Badajoz · Huelva · Cádiz · Jerez · Córdoba · Jaén · Granada · Guadix · Almería · Lorca · Cartagena · Murcia · Alicante · Elche · Albacete · Cuenca · Teruel · Castellón de la Plana · Tarragona · Lérida · Huesca · Pamplona · Logroño · Vitoria · San Sebastián · Biarritz · Bayonne · Pau · Tarbes · Narbonne · Béziers · Montpellier

Coimbra · Évora · Setúbal · Santarém · Braga · Algarve · Alto Alentejo · Baixo Alentejo · Beira Alta · Beira Baixa · Beira Litoral · Minho · Douro · Tras os Montes · Estremadura · Ribatejo

1 : 5 000 000

ICELAND
on the same scale
as general map

1 : 5 000 000

20 10 0   40   80   100 miles
40 20 0   40   80   120   160 km

East from Greenwich

Projection: Conical with two standard parallels

R.S.F.S.R.
1. Daghestan A.S.S.R.
2. Kabardino–Balkar A.S.S.R.
3. Mari A.S.S.R.
4. Mordovian A.S.S.R.
5. North Ossetian A.S.S.R.
6. Tatar A.S.S.R.
7. Udmurt A.S.S.R.
8. Chuvash A.S.S.R.
9. Checheno–Ingush A.S.S.R.
AZERBAIJAN
10. Nakhichevan A.S.S.R.
GEORGIA
11. Abkhaz A.S.S.R.
12. Adzhar A.S.S.R.

Projection: Conical Orthomorphic with two standard parallels

East from Greenwich

1 : 20 000 000

| 100 | 100 | 200 | 300 | 400 | 500 miles |
| 100 | 200 | 400 | 600 | 800 km |

O C E A N

Mys Dezhneva
(East C.)

Chukotskoye
More

Anadyrskiy Zaliv

St. Lawrence I.
(U.S.A.)

Ostrov Shmidt
Mys Arkticheskiy

Ostrov Komsomolets

Ostrov Oktyabrskoy Revolyutsii

Ostrov Pioner
965

Severnaya Zemlya

Ostrov Bolshevik

Proliv Vilkitskogo

Ostrov Vrangelya

Chukotskiy Khrebet

184.3

Koryakskiy Khrebet

Poluostrov Goryo Byrranga
Taymyr
1146

Upper Taymyr

Ostrov Bolshoy Begichev

Lapte v Novosibirskiye Ostrova
Sea

East Siberian Sea

Ostrov Medvezhi

1742

Sredinnyy

Bering Sea

Nordvik

Pyasina

Olenek

Tit-Ary

Tiksi

374

Lyakhovskiye Ostrova

Proliv Dmitriya Lapteva

Srednekolymsk

Kolyma

Okhotsko Kolymskoye

Gizhiginskaya Guba

Gizhiga

Penzhinskaya Guba

Poluostrov Kamchatka

3458
Petropavlovsk-Kamchatskiy

Gory Putorana
1701

962

Arctic Circle

Verkhoyansk
2389

Y A K U T S K

Verkhoyanskiy Khrebet

Khrebet Cherskogo
2662

2969

Magadan

Zaliv Shelikhova

1780

Sea of Okhotsk

Kamandarskiye Ostrova

Yakutsk

A S S R

S O C I A L I S T   R E P U B L I C

Okhotsk

Ostrov Bolshoy Shantar

Tatarskiy Proliv

Sakhalin

Nikolayevsk-na-Am.

2077

Yuzhno-Sakhalinsk

104

Vilyuysk

Olekminsk

Stanovoy Khrebet

Komsomolsk

Khrebet Sikhote Alin

Sovetskaya Gavan

Krasnoyarsk

Bratsk

Nizhneudinsk

Kirensk

2999

2840

Stanovoy Khrebet

Zeya

2840

Birobidzhan

Khabarovsk

Hokkaido
Sapporo

Hakodate

Cheremkhovo

Angarsk
1620

Ulan Ude

Chita

1530

Blagoveshchensk

Sretensk

Amur
(Manchuria)

Ussuriysk

Vladivostok
Nakhodka

Sea of JAPAN

Irkutsk
3491

Munku Sardyk

Hovsgol Nuur

Tsitsihar

Harbin

P e i

Kiamusze

Honshu

Sayan

Hangayn Nuruu

Ulaanbaatar
(Ulan Bator)

Hentiyn Nuruu

2800

Choybalsan

Tamsagbulag

Taonan

Tung
(Manchuria)

Kirin

Changchun
Szeping

2734

Chongjin

Sea of Japan

M O N G O L I A

G O B I

1949

Kingpeng

Chifeng

Fushun

Shenyang
(Mukden)

Anshan

North

Wonsan

Kanazawa

3957

Saynshand

D e s e r t

I n n e r   M o n g o l i a   R E P U B L I C

Tolun

Yingkow

Antung

Pyongyang

Soul

South

Toejon

Pusan

4925

Mingshui

Gashiun Nor

Chengteh

Changkiakow
(Kalgan)

Peiping
(Peking)

Lu-ta
Inchon

2400

Paotow

| Boundaries of U.S.S.R. |
| Boundaries of S.S.R. |
| Boundaries of A.S.S.R. |

COPYRIGHT. GEORGE PHILIP & SON. LTD.

1:50 000 000

250 0 250 500 750 1000 miles
250 0 500 1000 1500 km

1 : 20 000 000

100 0 100 200 300 400 500 miles
100 0 200 400 600 800 km

COPYRIGHT GEORGE PHILIP & SON LTD.

East from Greenwich

Projection: Alber's Equal Area with two standard parallels

1:20 000 000

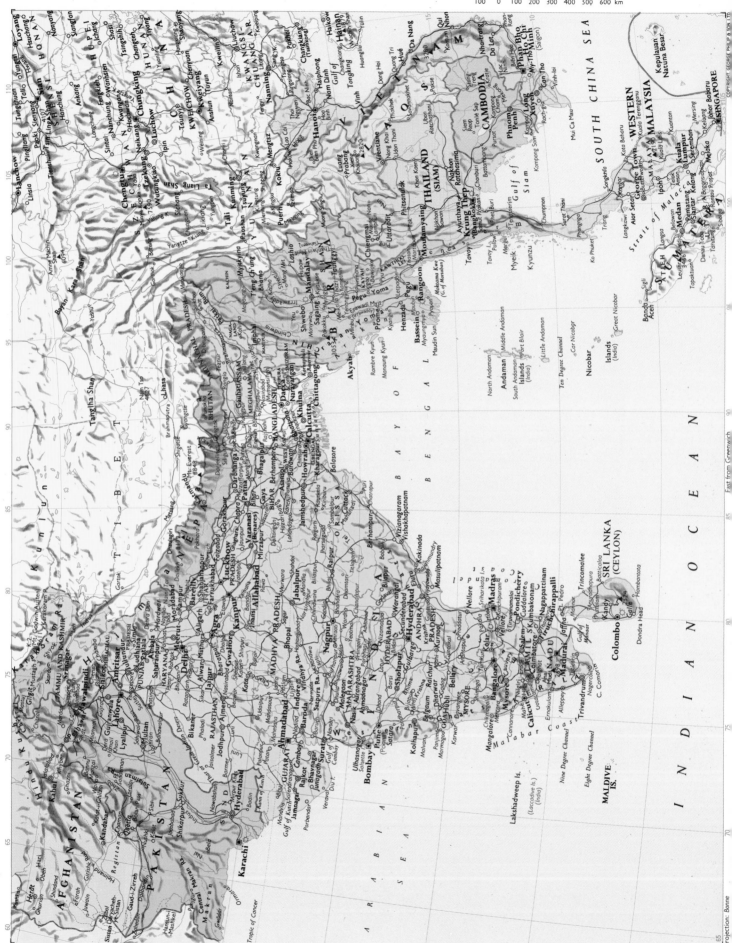

1:20 000 000

100   0   100   200   300   400   500 miles
100   0   200   400   600   800 km

P A C I F I C   O C E A N

Caroline Is.
Palau Is.

Caroline Islands

Caroline Islands
(U.S. Trust Territory)

Equator

Schouten
Japen
Geelvink B.
Manokwari
Vogelkop
I R I A N   J A Y A
Sorong
Wokam
Kobroor
Aru Is.
Trangan
Nuhutjut

Wessel Is.
Arnhem

A R A F U R A   S E A

Van Diemen
Darwin
AUSTRALIA

Waigeo
Gebe
Halmahera
Misool
Obi Is.
Ternate
Morotai

C E R A M   S E A
Ceram Is.
Banda Is.

B A N D A   S E A

Timor
Melville I.
Bathurst I.

T I M O R   S E A
Tanimbar Is.
Timor Laut
Yamdena
Selaru
Leti Is.

TAIWAN
(FORMOSA)
Bashi Channel

Kowloon
HONG KONG
(Br.)
Victoria
Macau
(Port.)

Pingsiang
Pakhoi
Changkiang
Kiungchow Str.
Haikow
Hainan
C. Bastion

Batan Is.
Babuyan Is.
Bashi Channel
Babuyan Chan.
Loog
Aparri
Babuyan Is.
2928
Baguio
L U Z O N
Quezon City
MANILA
Dagupan
Polillo Islands
Catanduanes
Lagonoy G.
Lamon B.
Sorsogon
S. Bernardino Str.
Samar
Masbate
Legaspi
Tacloban
Leyte
Calapan
Mindoro
Manila B.
Batangas
Calamian Group
Mindoro Str.
Panay
Tablas
Sibuyan
Iloilo
Negros
Cebu
Bacolod
Bohol
Ormoc
Surigao Strait
Buruan
C. S. Agustin

P H I L I P P I N E S

Palawan

S U L U   S E A

Cagayan
Zamboanga
Jolo
Sulu Arch.
Basilan
Moro Gulf
2965
Mindanao
Davao
Davao Gulf
Sarangani B.
Tinaca Point
Talaud
Gt. Sangi

Morotai
Moluccas
Talaud
Manado
Gorontalo
Kwandang
G. of Tomini
Peleng
Taliabu
Mangole
Banggai Arch.
Buru
Namlea
Ambon

S U L A W E S I
(C E L E B E S)
3455
Palu
Ujung Pandang
(Makasar)
Kendari
Butung
Salajar

C E L E B E S   S E A

Kuching
Kudat
Kota Kinabalu
(Jesselton)
Labuan
Victoria
Brunei
Miri
4101
Kinabalu
S A B A H
Sandakan
Darvel B.
Tawau
Tarakan

M A L A Y S I A
S A R A W A K
E A S T
Sibu
Kapuas Hulu
Samarinda
Balikpapan
Banjarmasin

B O R N E O
K A L I M A N T A N
Schwaner Ra.
Muller Ra.
Mahakam
Barito
Kapuas

S O U T H   C H I N A   S E A

Paracel Is.
Spratly

Pratas Is.

C. Bastion

Hanoi
Haiphong
G. of Tongking
Pakhoi
Thanh Hoa
Vinh
Ha Tinh
Quang Tri
Hué
Da-Nang
(Tourane)
V I E T -
N A M
An Nhon
Qui Nhon
Nha Trang
Phan Rang
Phan Thiet
Phan Bho Ho
(Saigon)
Go Cong
Can Tho

L A O S
Luang Prabang
Vientiane
Mekong

T H A I L A N D
(S I A M)
KRUNG THEP
(Bangkok)
Khorat
Nakhon Ratchasima
M. Ubon
Pakse
Srepok
Bien Hoa
CAMBODIA
PHNOM PENH
Battambang
Tonle Sap
Kg. Cham
Kratié
Kg. Thom

C. Cambodia

W E S T E R N   M A L A Y S I A
M A L A Y A
Kuala Lumpur
Seremban
Kuala Terengganu
Kota Baharu
Butterworth
George Town
Penang
Ipoh
Taiping
Port Kelang
Melaka
Johor Baharu
SINGAPORE

Natuna Is.
N. Natuna
S. Natuna
Anambas Is.
Tambelan Is.

Kuching
Pontianak
Kapuas

Riau Arch.
Lingga Arch.
Bangka
Palembang
Belitung
Karimata Is.

S U M A T R A
Medan
Pematangsiantar
Sibolga
Padang
Bukit Tinggi
Jambi
Pakanbaru
Teluk Betung

Nias
Mentawai Is.
Siberut
Sipora
Pagai
Enggano

Simeulue
Banda Aceh
(Kutaraja)

I N D O N E S I A

J A K A R T A
BANDUNG
Bogor
Semarang
SURABAJA
Surakarta
Jogjakarta
Malang
W E S T   J A V A   C E N T R A L   E A S T   J A V A
G r e a t e r   S u n d a   I s l a n d s
J a v a   S e a
Greater Sunda Is.

Bali
Lombok
Sumbawa
Flores
N u s a   T e n g g a r a   (L e s s e r   S u n d a   I s l a n d s)
F L O R E S   S E A
Sumba (Sandalwood)
Sawu
S a w u   S e a

B U R M A
RANGOON
Bassein
Prome
Moulmein
Amherst
Tavoy
Mergui
Mergui Arch.
Chiangmai
Tak
(Raheng)
Mt. Phitsanulok
Ayutthya
Nakhon Sawan
Chanthaburi
Phanom Dang Raek
Nakhon Si Thammarat
Songkhla
(Singora)
Pattani
Trang
Phuket
Isthmus of Kra
Chumphon
Point Bai Bung
G u l f   o f   S i a m
Con Son Is.

Ramree
Cheduba I.
Middle Andaman
Andaman Islands
(India)
Pt. Blair
Little Andaman
Ten Degree Channel
Car Nicobar
Nicobar Islands
(India)
Great Nicobar

A N D A M A N   S E A

S t r a i t   o f   M a l a c c a

I N D I A N   O C E A N

Christmas I.
(Austral.)

Cocos or Keeling Is.
(Austral.)

Equator

East from Greenwich

Projection: Bonne

SEA OF JAPAN

Oki-Shotō

CHŪGOKU
SHIMANE
Matsue · Tottori
Izumo · Yonago
Hamada
Masuda
Hagi
YAMAGUCHI
Shimonoseki
KITAKYŪSHŪ
Fukuoka
SAGA
Karatsu
Imari
Sasebo
NAGASAKI
Nagasaki
Ōmura · Isahaya
Ōmuta · Kumamoto
KUMAMOTO
Yatsushiro
Minamata
KYŪSHŪ
MIYAZAKI
Sendai
KAGOSHIMA
Kagoshima
Nichinan
Miyazaki
Nobeoka
Ōita · OITA
Beppu
Hiroshima · HIROSHIMA
Kurashiki
Okayama · OKAYAMA
Fukuyama
Kure
Iwakuni
Tokuyama
Matsuyama · EHIME
Uwajima
SHIKOKU
KŌCHI
Kōchi
Tosa-Wan
Takamatsu · KAGAWA
Tokushima · TOKUSHIMA
Marugame · Sakaide

KŌBE · OSAKA · Higashiōsaka
Amagasaki
HYOGO · Nishinomiya
Akashi
NARA · Nara
WAKAYAMA · Wakayama
KYŌTO
Ōtsu
NAGOYA
Gifu · GIFU
Ichinomiya
Toyota · AICHI
Okazaki
Hamamatsu
Shizuoka · SHIZUOKA
Numazu
TOKYO
YOKOHAMA
Kawasaki
Chiba · CHIBA
Yokosuka
Odawara
Atami
Fuji
Mishima

TOKAIDO LINE

PACIFIC OCEAN

East from Greenwich

1 : 5 000 000
25   0   25   50   75   100 miles
25   0   50   100   km
Projection: Conical with two standard parallels

Yaku-shima
Ōsumi-Shotō
Tane-ga-Shima
Ōsumi-Kaikyō

SOUTH KOREA
Chungju
Taejŏn
Kunsan · Iri
Chŏnju
Taegu
Kwangju
Mokpo
PUSAN
Masan
Yosu · Sunchŏn
Korea-Kaikyō
Tsushima

HOKKAIDO
Sea of Okhotsk
Rebun-Tō
Rishiri-Tō
Wakkanai
Sōya-Misaki
Abashiri
Asahikawa
Sapporo
Otaru
Muroran
Hakodate
Aomori
Hirosaki
Hachinohe
Morioka
Akita
Sendai
Yamagata
Niigata
Kōriyama
Fukushima
Iwaki
Utsunomiya
Mito
TOKYO
YOKOHAMA
Nagoya
Shizuoka
Hamamatsu

SEA OF JAPAN

TŌHOKU

Noto-Hantō
Toyama
Kanazawa
CHŪBU
KANTŌ
KINKI

PACIFIC OCEAN

East from Greenwich

1 : 10 000 000
100 50 0   50 100 150 200 miles
100   0   100   200   300 km
Projection: Bonne

Continuation Southwards on same scale

Tokara-Kaikyō
Tokara-Shima
Suwanose-Jima
Nansei-Shotō
Amami-Ō-Shima
Toku-no-Shima
Ōsumi-Shotō
Tane-ga-Shima
Yaku-Shima

REFERENCE TO PREFECTURES

HOKKAIDO DISTRICT	KINKI DISTRICT
1 Hokkaidō	24 Hyogo
TŌHOKU DISTRICT	25 Kyōto
2 Aomori	26 Shiga
3 Akita	27 Ōsaka
4 Iwate	28 Nara
5 Yamagata	29 Mie
6 Miyagi	30 Wakayama
7 Fukushima	**CHŪGOKU DISTRICT**
CHŪBU DISTRICT	31 Tottori
8 Niigata	32 Okayama
9 Ishikawa	33 Shimane
10 Toyama	34 Hiroshima
11 Fukui	35 Yamaguchi
12 Gifu	**SHIKOKU DISTRICT**
13 Nagano	36 Kagawa
14 Yamanashi	37 Tokushima
15 Aichi	38 Ehime
	39 Kōchi
KANTO DISTRICT	**KYŪSHŪ DISTRICT**
17 Gumma	40 Fukuoka
18 Tochigi	41 Saga
19 Saitama	42 Nagasaki
20 Ibaraki	43 Kumamoto
21 Tōkyō	44 Ōita
22 Chiba	45 Miyazaki
23 Kanagawa	46 Kagoshima

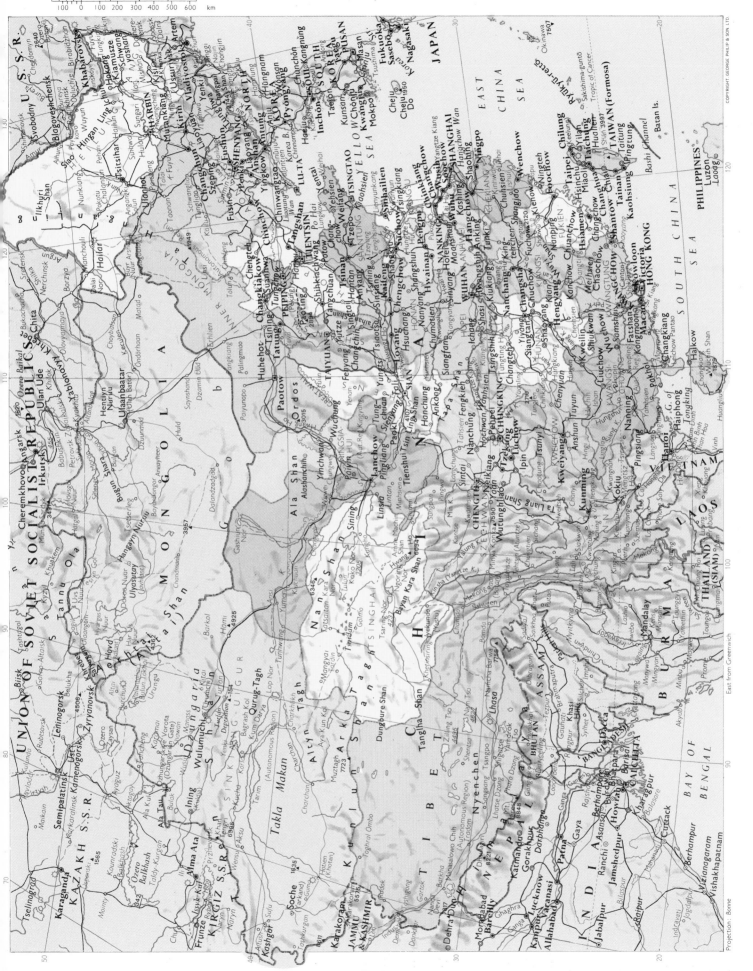

1:20 000 000

COPYRIGHT GEORGE PHILIP & SON LTD

East from Greenwich

Projection: Bonne

TIMOR SEA

INDIAN OCEAN

WESTERN AUSTRALIA

NORTHERN TERRITORY

SOUTH AUS

Ashmore Reef
Cartier I.
Scott Reef
Rowley Shoals

Croker
Cobourg Pen.
Melville I.
Van Diemen Gulf
Bathurst I.
Clarence Str.
P. Darwin
Darwin
Pt. Blaze
Anson B.
C. Ford
Batchelor
Rum Jungle
Goulburn Is.
Junction B.
Crocodile I.
Elc
Castlereagh B.
Buckingham B.
Arnh
Arnhem Land

C. Londonderry
C. Talbot
Vansittart B.
C. Bougainville
Admiralty G.
Montague Sd.
York Sd.
Bonaparte Archipelago
Brunswick B.
Koolan & Cockatoo Is.
Collier B.
King Sd.
C. Lévêque
Lacepede Is.
C. Baskerville
Carnot B.
C. Boileau
Broome
C. Latouche Treville
C. Bossut
Roebuck B.
La Grange
Dampier Downs

Jos. Bonaparte Gulf
Cambridge G.
Queens Chan.
Drysdale
Wyndham
Mt. Hann 776
Kimberley
King Leopold Ras.
Mt. Ord 936
Glenroy
Meda
Derby
Fitzroy
Fitzroy Crossing
Hall's Creek
Durack Range
Ord
DUNCAN
Gulf Basin
Kununurra
Victoria
Gordon Downs
GREAT NORTHERN

Frances Creek
Pine Creek
Katherine
Roper
Mataranka
Larrimah
Birdum
Victoria River Downs
Wave Hill
Newcastle Waters
L. Woods
Powell Creek
Renner Springs T.O.
Tennant Creek
Barkl

Daly
Daly Waters

Eighty Mile Beach
P. Hedland
Finucane I.
Cape Lambert
De Grey
Nimingarra
Mount Goldsworthy
Marble Bar
Throssell Ra.
L. Blanche
L. Dora
Canning Basin
Great Sandy Desert
Gregory Lake

Sturt
Hordern Hills
The Granites
Tanami Desert

NORTHE
TERRITO

Dampier Archipelago
Hampton Harb.
Monte Bello Is.
Barrow I.
C. Preston
C. Dampier
Roebourne
Pilbara
Yule
Shaw
Fortescue
Hamersley Ra.
Wittenoom
Mt. Bruce
Mt. Enid
Mt. Tom Price 1227
Mt. Meharry 1251
Ophthalmia Ra.
Ashburton
Parraburdoo
Mount Whaleback
Newman
Mt. Nicholas
Robertson Ra.
Nullagine
L. Disappointment

Deepdale
Onslow
N.W. Cape
Exmouth G.
Learmonth
Pt. Cloates
Exmouth
N.W. COASTAL

Mt. Singleton 844
Barrow Creek T.O.
Sand
Mt. Freeling 998
Reynolds Ra.
Mt. Laughlen
Mt. Liebig 1510
Mt. Ziel
Mt. Macdonald 1524
L. Macdonald
Macdonnell Ras.
Mt. Laughlen 1169
Alice Springs
James Ra.
Palmer
Finke
Hugh
S
D
Charlot Water

L. Mackay

Gibson Desert
Rawlinson Ra.
L. Amadeus
Mt. Olga 1069
Ayers Rock 867
Blackstone Ra.
Barrow Ra.
Musgrave Ranges
Mt. Woodroffe 1440
Hamilton
Alberga
Everard Ras.
Oodnadatta

C. Farquhar
L. McLeod
C. Cuvier
Geographe Chan.
Bernier I.
Dorre I.
Naturaliste Chan.
Dirk Hartog
Denham
S. Passage
Steep Pt.
North West Basin
Barlee Ra.
Mt. Augustus 1105
Mt. Egerton 994
Lyons
Gascoyne
Wooramel
Carnarvon
Shark B.
GREAT NORTHERN

Peak Hill
Robinson Ras.
L. Buchanan
L. Carnegie
L. Wells 661
L. Yeo
Great Victoria Desert
Cooper Pedy
L. Maurice
Stuar

Gantheaume B.
P. Gregory
Houtman Abrolhos
Northampton
Champion B.
Geraldton
Dongara
Murchison
Sanford
Meekatharra
Nannine
Cue
L. Austin
Sandstone
Mt. Magnet
Tallering Peak 453
Yalgoo
Mullewa
L. Monger
L. Barlee
L. Moore
L. Raeside
L. Ballard
Leonora
Malcolm
Menzies
Laverton
L. Rason
L. Carey
L. Minigwal

SOUTH AUS
Maralinga
Oodlea
Tarcoola
L. Harris
L. Everard
Penong
Ceduna
Nukey
Ga
L. Gair

Jurien B.
Wedge I.
Coastal
Plains
Basin
GERALDTON
Bonnie Rock
Bencubbin
Kalgoorlie
Coolgardie
Boulder
Kanowna
Zanthus
Southern Cross
Bullfinch
Merredin
Kellerberrin
The Johnston Lakes
Norseman
L. Lefroy
L. Cowan
L. Dundas
Premier Downs
Rawlinna
Forrest
Deakin
Eucla Basin
Nullarbor Plain
Hampton Tableland
Eyre
Eucla Motel
Head of Bight
Pt. Dover
Pt. Culver
Rocky Pt.
C. Adieu
Fowlers B.
Nuyts Archipelago
C. Radstock
Streaky B.
Anxious B.
Investigator Group

Midland Junction
Perth
Fremantle
Kwinana
Swan
York
Northam
GREAT EASTERN
Beverley
Brookton
Narrogin
Newdegate
Pinjarra
Bunbury
Collie
Geographe B.
Busselton
C. Naturaliste
Augusta
C. Leeuwin
Bridgetown
Manjimup
Pemberton
Katanning
Wagin
Nyabing
Gnowangerup
Stirling Ra.
Mt. Barker
Albany
Denmark
Tor B.
King George Sound
Pt. d'Entrecasteaux
Pt. Nuyts
ALBANY
Ravensthorpe
Hopetoun
Esperance
Doubtful B.
Pt. Hood
C. Knob
C. Arid
Archipelago of the Recherche
C. le Grand
C. Pasley
Esperance B.
Great Australian Bight
Coffin B. Penin.
Whidbey Is.
Port Lin
C. Catastroph
This
Ey
Pe

NEW ZEALAND & DEPENDENCIES
1:60 000 000

200 0 200 400 600 800 miles
200 0 400 800 1200 km
- - - - - New Zealand Territory

SAMOA ISLANDS
1:12 000 000

FIJI AND TONGA ISLANDS
1:12 000 000

50 0 50 100 150 miles
50 0 50 100 150 200 250 km

1:6 000 000

20 0 20 40 60 80 100 miles
20 0 40 80 120 160 km

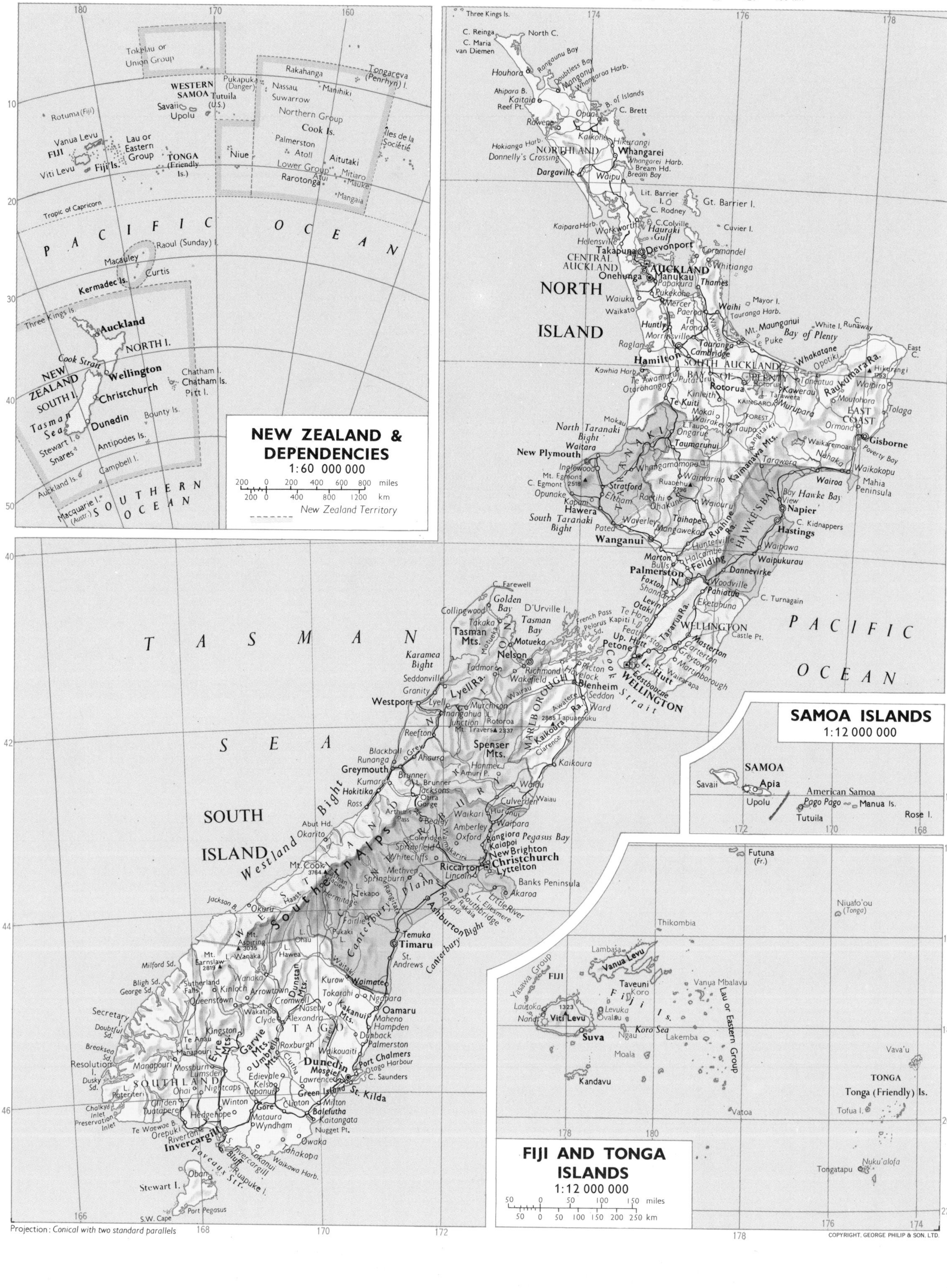

NORTH ISLAND

SOUTH ISLAND

PACIFIC OCEAN

TASMAN SEA

SOUTHERN OCEAN

WESTERN SAMOA

FIJI

TONGA (Friendly) Is.

Cook Is.

Northern Group

Lower Group

Tropic of Capricorn

NEW ZEALAND

Auckland
Wellington
Christchurch
Dunedin

SAMOA
Apia
Savaii
Upolu
American Samoa
Pago Pago
Tutuila
Manua Is.
Rose I.

FIJI
Suva
Viti Levu
Vanua Levu
Taveuni
Lau or Eastern Group
Koro Sea
Lakemba
Kandavu

TONGA
Tonga (Friendly) Is.
Nuku'alofa
Tongatapu
Vava'u

Projection: Conical with two standard parallels

COPYRIGHT. GEORGE PHILIP & SON. LTD.

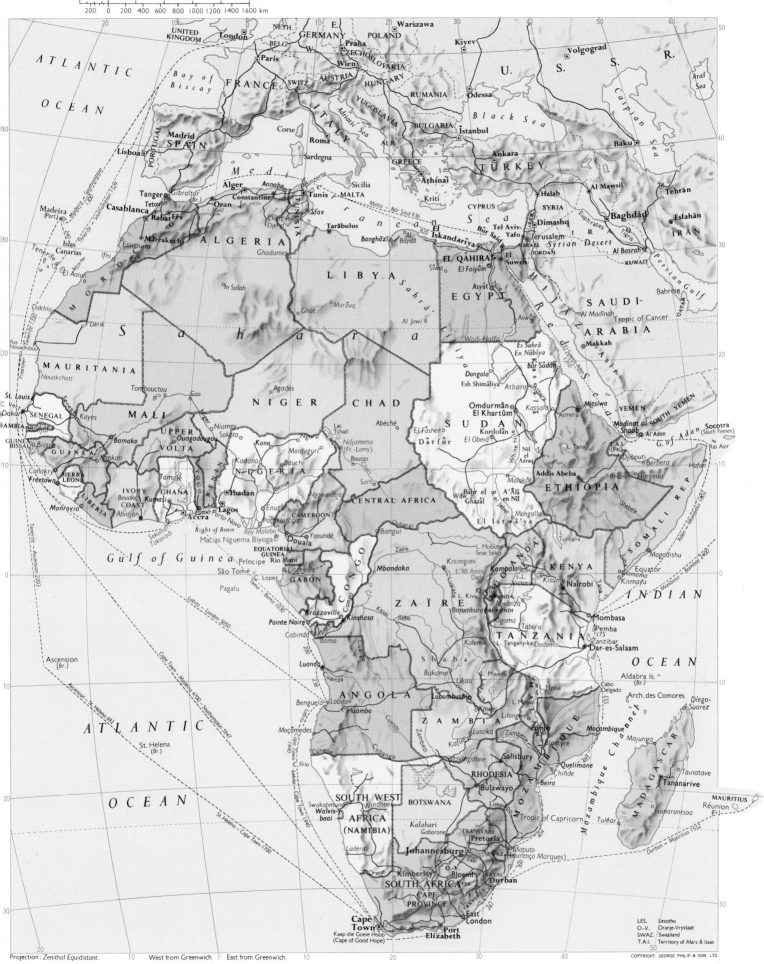

1:40 000 000

200   0   200   400   600   800   1000 miles
200   0   200 400 600 800 1000 1200 1400 1600 km

Projection: Zenithal Equidistant.   West from Greenwich | East from Greenwich   COPYRIGHT. GEORGE PHILIP & SON. LTD.

LES.   Lesotho
O.-V.   Oranje-Vrystaat
SWAZ.   Swaziland
T.A.I.   Territory of Afars & Issas

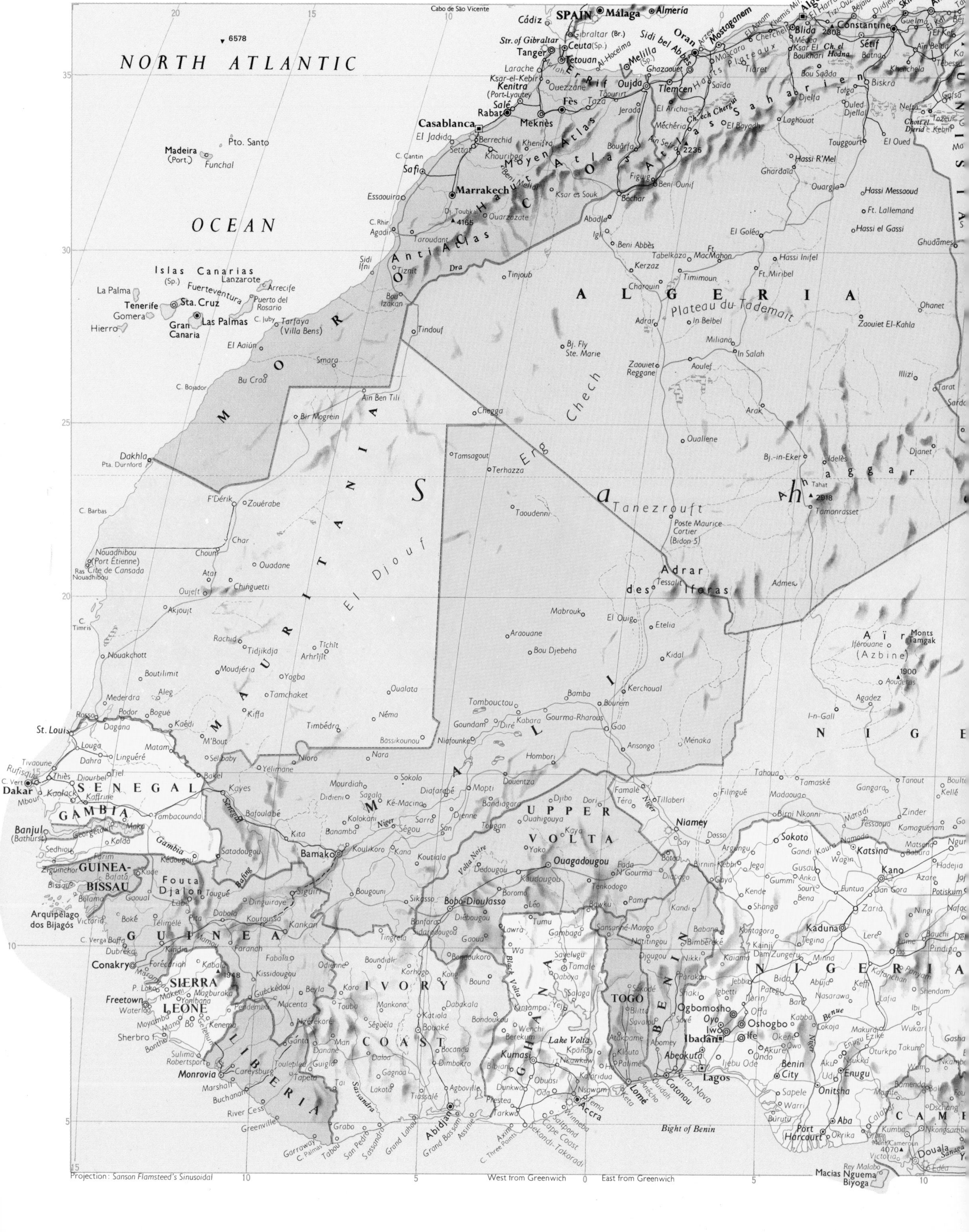
NORTH ATLANTIC
OCEAN
Cabo de São Vicente
SPAIN
Málaga
Almería
Cádiz
Gibraltar (Br.)
Str. of Gibraltar
Ceuta (Sp.)
Tanger
Tetouan
Al-Hoceima
Melilla (Sp.)
Sidi bel Abbès
Oran
Arzew
Mostaganem
Alger (Algiers)
El Harrach
Tizi-Ouzou
Bejaïa
Djidjelli
Skikda
Annaba
Blida
Médéa
Constantine
Sétif
Guelma
Batna
Biskra
Khenchela
Tébessa
Larache
Ksar-el-Kebir
Kenitra (Port-Lyautey)
Ouezzane
Rif
Oujda
Ghazaouet
Tlemcen
Saïda
Tiaret
Mascara
Hauts Plateaux
Salé
Rabat
Fès
Taza
Taourirt
Jerada
El Aricha
Chott Chergui
Ch. el Hodna
Bou Saâda
Djelfa
Laghouat
Casablanca
Meknès
Khenifra
Mécheria
El Bayadh
Aïn Sefra
2235
El Jadida
Berrechid
Settat
Khouribga
Moyen Atlas
Beni Mellal
Haut Atlas
Atlas Saharien
C. Cantin
Safi
Marrakech
Essaouira
Dj. Toubkal
4165
Ouarzazate
Ksar es Souk
Bougtia
Figuig
Beni-Ounif
Béchar
Abadla
Igli
Beni Abbès
Ghardaïa
Hassi R'Mel
Ouargla
Touggourt
El Oued
Hassi Messaoud
Ft. Lallemand
Hassi el Gassi
Ghudāmes
El Goléa
Nefta
Tozeur
Chott el Djerid
Kebili
Tunisia
Madeira (Port.)
Pto. Santo
Funchal
6578
C. Rhir
Agadir
Taroudant
Anti Atlas
Sidi Ifni
Tiznit
Dra
Tinjoub
Bou Izakan
Islas Canarias (Sp.)
Lanzarote
Fuerteventura
Arrecife
Puerto del Rosario
La Palma
Tenerife
Sta. Cruz
Gomera
Las Palmas
Hierro
Gran Canaria
C. Juby
Tarfaya (Villa Bens)
Tindouf
El Aaiún
Smara
Bu Craa
C. Bojador
Aïn Ben Tili
Bir Mogrein
Chegga
Tabelkoza
Ft. MacMahon
Hassi Inifel
Kerzaz
Timimoun
Ft. Miribel
Charouin
ALGERIA
Plateau du Tademait
Ohanet
Adrar
In Belbel
Zaouiet El-Kahla
Bj. Fly Ste. Marie
Miliana
In Salah
Zaouiet Reggane
Aoulef
Illizi
Tarat
Erg Chech
Arak
Sardo
Dakhla
Pta. Durnford
Ouallene
Bj.-in-Eker
Idelès
Djanet
Tamsagout
Terhazza
Ahaggar
Tahat
2918
Tamanrasset
C. Barbas
F'Dérik
Zouérabe
Taoudenni
Tanezrouft
Poste Maurice Cortier (Bidon 5)
Sahara
Char
Choum
Nouadhibou (Port Étienne)
Ras Nouadhibou
Cité de Cansada
Ouadane
El Djouf
Atar
Chinguetti
Oujeft
Adrar des Iforas
Tessalit
Admer
Akjoujt
C. Timris
MAURITANIA
Mabrouk
El Ouig
Etelia
Araouane
Aïr (Azbine)
Monts Tamgak
Iférouane
Rachid
Tidjikdja
Tichit
Arhrijit
Bou Djebeha
Kidal
1900
Aouderas
Nouakchott
Boutilimit
Moudjéria
Yogba
Kerchoual
Aleg
Tamchaket
Oualata
Bamba
Bourem
Agadez
Mederdra
Kiffa
Tombouctou
Rosso
Podor
Bogué
Kaédi
Néma
Goundam
Diré
Kabara
Gourma-Rharous
In-Gall
St. Louis
Dagana
M'Bout
Timbédra
Bassikounou
Niafounké
Gao
MALI
NIGER
Louga
Matam
Dahra
Linguéré
Selibaby
Nioro
Nara
Hombori
Ansongo
Ménaka
Tivaoune
Rufisque
C. Vert
Dakar
Thiès
Diourbel
Tiel
Bakel
Yélimané
Kayes
Mbour
Kaolack
Kaffrine
SENEGAL
Mourdiah
Sokolo
Diafarabé
Mopti
Douentza
Famalé
Téra
Tillaberi
Tahoua
Tamaské
Tanout
Gangara
Diébéni
Sagala
Ké-Macina
Bandiagara
Djibo
Dori
Filingué
Madaoua
Kellé
GAMBIA
Tambacounda
Bafoulabé
Kolokani
Sarro
Djenne
Ouahigouya
UPPER VOLTA
Niamey
Birni Nkonni
Maradi
Zinder
Banjul (Bathurst)
Georgetown
Maka
Kolda
Banamba
Ségou
San
Tougan
Kaya
Dosso
Say
Tessaoua
Kamaguénam
Sedhiou
Gambia
Satadougou
Kita
Bamako
Koulikoro
Kana
Koutiala
Yako
Volta Noire
Ouagadougou
Fada N'Gourma
Botou
Birnin-Kebbi
Argungu
Sokoto
Gandi
Katsina
Ziguinchor
GUINEA-BISSAU
Bafatá
Bissau
Bolama
Gaoual
Kédougou
Fouta Djalon
Labé
Tougué
Bafing
Siguiri
Bougouni
Sikasso
Dédougou
Koudougou
Tenkodogo
Diapaga
Gaya
Jega
Gusau
Anka
Kano
Hadejia
Azare
Potiskum
Arquipélago dos Bijagós
Boké
Télimélé
Pita
Dabola
Dinguiraye
Kouroussa
Kankan
Bobo-Dioulasso
Boromo
Léo
Pama
Kende
Gummi
Sokoto
Bena
Funtua
Dan Gora
C. Verga
Boffa
Dubréka
GUINEA
Kindia
Faranah
Banfora
Diébougou
Gaoua
Tingréla
Tumu
Lawra
Gambaga
Sansanné-Mango
Kandi
Shanga
Zaria
Ningi
Conakry
Forécariah
Kabala
1948
Fabala
Odienné
Boundiali
Wa
Navrongo
Natitingou
Babana
Bimbéréké
Kontagora
Kaduna
Lere
Bauchi
Pindiga
Jos
P. Loko
Makeni
Magburaka
Kissidougou
Korhogo
Bondoukoro
Kong
Bouna
Savelugu
Tamale
Daboya
Djougou
Nikki
Kaiama
Kainji
Dam
Zungeru
Minna
SIERRA LEONE
Freetown
Waterloo
Yonibana
Guéckédou
Macenta
Beyla
Black Volta
Salaga
Parakou
Jebba
Bida
Abuja
Keffi
Kafanchan
Shendam
Lafia
Moyamba
Bo
Kenema
Pendembu
Nzérékoré
Touba
Dabakala
Mankono
IVORY COAST
Séguéla
Katiola
Bouaké
Kintampo
Yeji
GHANA
TOGO
Sokodé
Bassari
Blitta
Savalou
Shaki
Ogbomosho
Oyo
Iwo
Ilorin
Offa
Oshogbo
Ife
Ibadan
Patogi
Baro
Nasarawa
Kabba
Benue
Lokoja
Makurdi
Wukari
Sherbro I.
Bonthe
Sulima
Robertsport
Monrovia
Careysburg
LIBERIA
Ganta
Danané
Man
Guiglo
Toulepleu
Tapeta
Daloa
Bondoukou
Wenchi
Berekum
Lake Volta
Kpandu
Atakpamé
Kluoto
Palimé
BENIN
Abomey
Abeokuta
Ijebu Ode
Okene
Owo
Akure
Ondo
Enugu Ezike
Oturkpo
Takum
Gasha
Marshall
Buchanan
River Cess
Greenville
Tai
Sassandra
Gagnoa
Lakota
Dimbokro
Bocanda
Agboville
Tiassalé
Bibiani
Kumasi
Obuasi
Nkawkaw
Koforidua
Dunkwa
Oda
Nsawam
Keta
Lomé
Anécho
Ouidah
Cotonou
Porto-Novo
Lagos
Benin City
Auchi
Akwu
Udi
Nsukka
Enugu
Onitsha
Sapele
Warri
Burutu
Aba
Port Harcourt
Okrika
Calabar
Bamenda
Kumba
CAMEROON
Grabo
Tabou
C. Palmas
Garraway
San Pedro
Grand Lahou
Abidjan
Grand Bassam
Assinie
Axim
C. Three Points
Sekondi-Takoradi
Cape Coast
Saltpond
Winneba
Accra
Tema
Prestea
Tarkwa
Bight of Benin
Buea
Victoria
4070
Mt. Cameroun
Douala
Edéa
Sanaga
Macias Nguema Biyoga
Rey Malabo
Projection: Sanson Flamsteed's Sinusoidal
West from Greenwich
East from Greenwich
20
15
10
5
0
35
30
25

1:15 000 000

100 0 100 200 300 400 miles
100 0 100 200 300 400 500 600 km

MEDITERRANEAN SEA

MALTA
Lampedusa (It.)
Pantelleria (It.)
Sicilia
C. Passero
Ragusa

TURKEY
Antalya
Ródhos
Karpathos
Kríti
Iraklion

CYPRUS
Levkosía (Nicosia)
Lemesós

SYRIA
Al Mawsil (Mosul)
Halab
Hamā
Homs
Dimashq (Damascus)

LEBANON
Bayrūt
ISRAEL
Tel Aviv-Yafo
Haifa
Jerusalem (Al Quds)
Amman
JORDAN
IRAQ
Ar Rutbah
Bādiyat ash Shām
Mesopotamia
Nahr Dijla (Tigris)
Nahr al Furat

TARĀBULUS (Tripoli)
Banghāzī (Benghazi)
LIBYA
Barqa (Cyrenaica)
Sahrâ'
Lîbîya
Fezzan
Tibesti
Borkou
Ennedi
Erg du Djourab

EGYPT
EL QÂHIRA (Cairo)
El Iskandarîya (Alexandria)
El Gîza
El Faiyûm
Beni Suef
El Minyâ
Asyût
Sohâg
Qena
El Uqsur (Luxor)
Aswân
Aswân High Dam
Buheiret en Naser (Lake Nasser)
Es Sahrâ' esh Sharqîya
Sinai
Suez
Tropic of Cancer

SAUDI ARABIA
HIJAZ
An Nafūd
Tabūk
Madā'in Salih
Al Madīnah
Makkah (Mecca)
Jiddah
RED SEA

SUDAN
El Khartûm (Khartoum)
Omdurmân
ESH SHAMALîYA
AN NîL
BAHR EL AHMAR
Bûr Sûdân (Port Sudan)
SHAMÂL DÂRFÛR
JANUB DÂRFÛR
SHAMÂL KORDOFÂN
JANUB KORDOFÂN
El Obeid
El Fâsher
Nyâlâ
BAHR EL GHAZÂL
A'ÂLÂ EN NîL
AN NîL EL ABYAD
AN NîL EL AZRAQ
EL ISTWÂ'YA
Jûba
Wad Medani
Kassala

CHAD
Ndjamena (Ft. Lamy)
Lac Tchad
Abéché

CENTRAL AFRICA
Bangui
ZAÏRE (CONGO)

ETHIOPIA
Addis Abeba (Addis Ababa)
L. Tana
L. Abaya
L. Shamo

ERITREA
Asmera
Mitsiwa

KENYA
L. Turkana

COPYRIGHT. GEORGE PHILIP & SON. LTD.

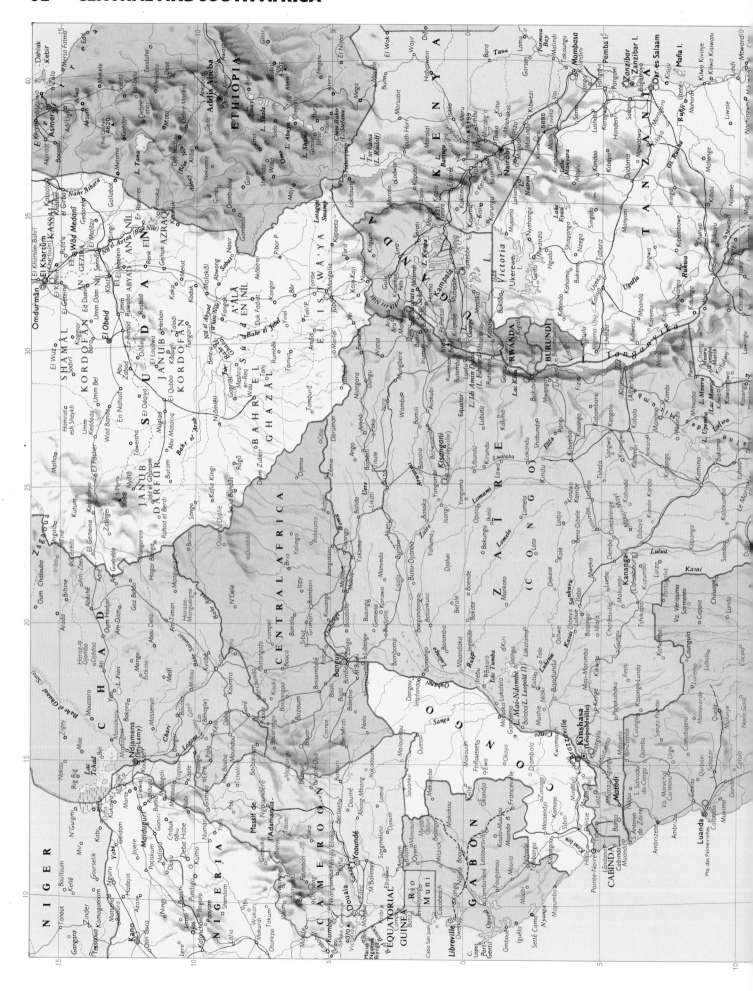

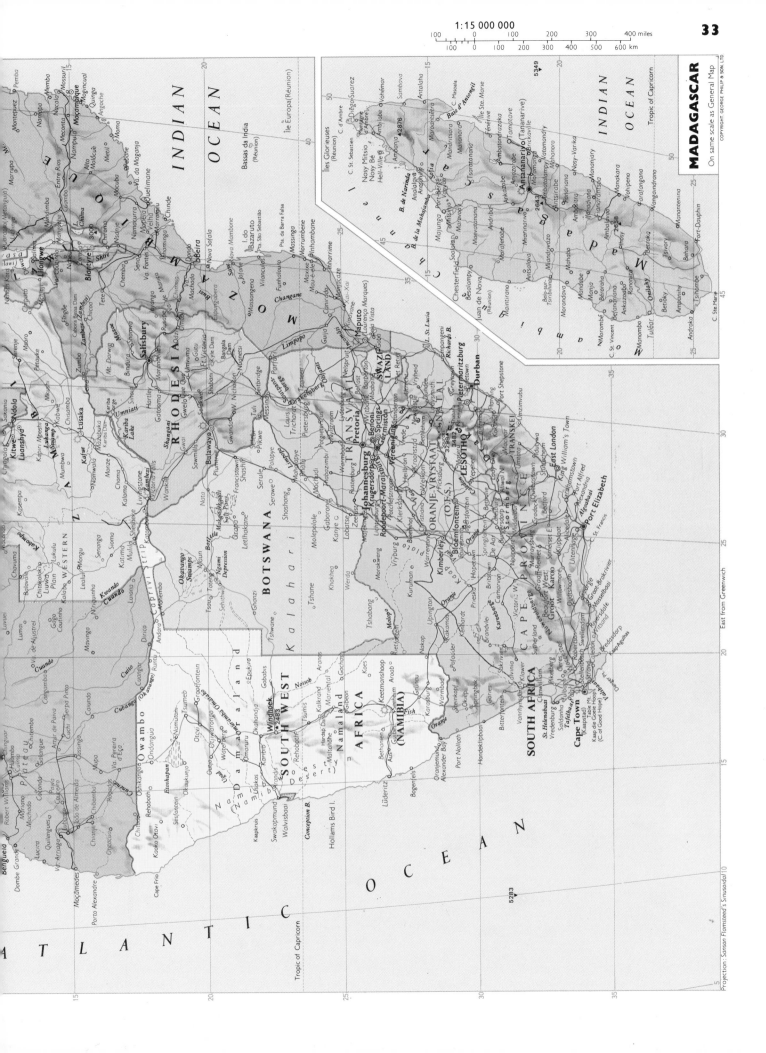

1:15 000 000

100   0   100   200   300   400 miles
100 0 100 200 300 400 500 600 km

MADAGASCAR
On same scale as General Map

COPYRIGHT GEORGE PHILIP & SON LTD.

INDIAN OCEAN

INDIAN OCEAN

ATLANTIC OCEAN

Tropic of Capricorn

Tropic of Capricorn

East from Greenwich

Projection: Sanson Flamsteed's Sinusoidal

RHODESIA

BOTSWANA

Kalahari

SOUTH WEST AFRICA (NAMIBIA)

SOUTH AFRICA

CAPE PROVINCE

TRANSVAAL

NATAL

ORANJE-VRYSTAAT (O.F.S.)

SWAZILAND

LESOTHO

TRANSKEI

Cape Town

Port Elizabeth

East London

Durban

Johannesburg

Pretoria

Salisbury

Bulawayo

Lusaka

Maputo

Beira

Windhoek

Walvisbaai

Antananarivo (Tananarive)

1:15 000 000

100 50 0   100   200   300   400 miles
100   0   100   200   300   400   500   600 km

ATLANTIC

GREENLAND

Baffin Bay

Davis Strait

Cumberland Peninsula

Hudson Strait

Foxe Channel

Southampton I.

Hudson Bay

Ungava Bay

Ungava Peninsula

James Bay

LABRADOR

NEWFOUNDLAND

QUEBEC

St. John's

Gulf of St. Lawrence

PR. EDWARD I.

NEW BRUNSWICK

NOVA SCOTIA

Halifax

MONTRÉAL

Québec

Ottawa

Trois Rivières

TORONTO

London

Buffalo

DETROIT

Cleveland

NEW YORK

NEW JERSEY

Boston

Providence

MAINE

NEW HAMPSHIRE

VERMONT

NEW YORK

MASS.

CONN.

PENNSYLVANIA

OHIO

INDIANA

Lake Superior

Lake Huron

Lake Ontario

Lake Erie

ATLANTIC OCEAN

West from Greenwich   COPYRIGHT. GEORGE PHILIP & SON. LTD.

HAWAII
1:10 000 000

20 0 20 40 60 80 miles
20 0 40 80 120 km

Projection: Albers' Equal Area with two standard parallels

West from Greenwich

1:12 000 000

50   0   50   100   150   200   250   300 miles
50 0 50 100 150 200 250 300 350 400 450 km

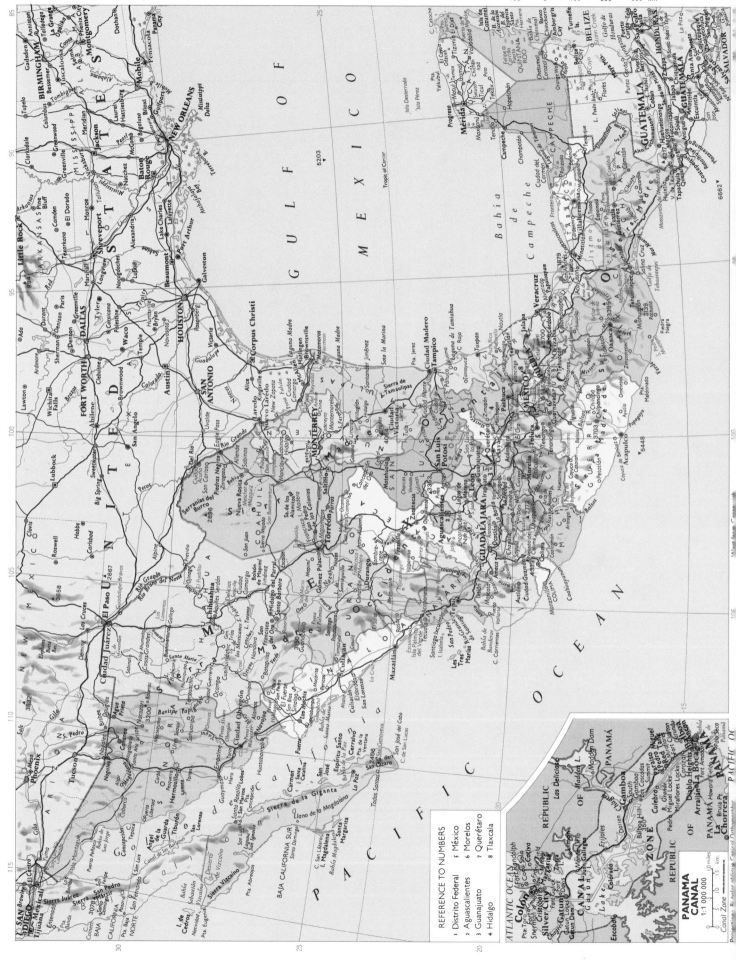

1:12 000 000

REFERENCE TO NUMBERS
1 Distrito Federal   5 México
2 Aguascalientes   6 Morelos
3 Guanajuato   7 Querétaro
4 Hidalgo   8 Tlaxcala

PANAMA CANAL
1:1 000 000

1:12 000 000

100   0   100   200 miles
100   0   100   200   300 km

BERMUDA
1:1 000 000
0   5 miles
0   8 km

St. George's
St. David's I.
The Castle Harb.
Flatts Tucker's Town
Ireland I. North Village
Somerset Spanish Point Hamilton

LEEWARD ISLANDS
1:8 000 000

Anguilla
St. Martin (Fr.)
St. Maarten (Neth.)
Saba I. St. Barthélemy (Fr.)
St. Eustatius (Neth.)
Bassetterre St. Christopher (St. Kitts)
Nevis Redonda
Charlestown Montserrat
Plymouth
GUADELOUPE (Fr.)
Basse Terre Ste. Rose
Grand Bourg
Les Saintes Marie-Galante (Fr.)
Barbuda
St. John's Antigua (Br.)
Falmouth
Le Moule
Pointe-à-Pitre
Dominica
Roseau (Br.)
Portsmouth

JAMAICA
1:8 000 000

Montego Bay
Falmouth
KINGSTON
Spanish Town
Morant Point
Port Morant

TRINIDAD & TOBAGO
1:8 000 000

Port of Spain
TRINIDAD
San Fernando
Tobago

WINDWARD ISLANDS
1:8 000 000

MARTINIQUE
Fort-de-France
St. Lucia
Castries
Soufrière
St. Vincent
Kingstown
The Grenadines
Bequia
Mustique
Carriacou
GRENADA
St. George's

BARBADOS
Speightstown
Bridgetown

GULF OF MEXICO

FLORIDA
Sarasota
Fort Myers
West Palm Beach
Fort Lauderdale
MIAMI
Key West
Florida Keys

BAHAMAS
Grand Bahama
Little Abaco I.
Great Abaco I.
Bimini Is.
Nassau
New Providence
Andros Island
GREAT BAHAMA BANK
Eleuthera I.
Cat I.
San Salvador (Watling I., Guanahani)
Long I.
Crooked I.
Acklins I.
Mayaguana I.
Great Inagua I.
Little Inagua I.
Caicos Islands (Br.)
Turks I. (Br.)

MEXICO
Isla de Cozumel

CUBA
Pinar del Rio
La Habana
Matanzas
Cárdenas
Santa Clara
Cienfuegos
Sancti Spíritus
Camagüey
Ciego de Ávila
Holguín
Santiago de Cuba
Guantánamo

CAYMAN ISLANDS (Br.)
Grand Cayman

HAITI
Port-au-Prince
Cap-Haïtien

DOMINICAN REP.
Santo Domingo
Santiago

HISPANIOLA

PUERTO RICO (U.S.A.)
San Juan
Ponce
Mayagüez

Virgin Is. (U.S.A.) (Br.)
Anegada
St. Croix

ATLANTIC OCEAN

CARIBBEAN SEA

GREATER ANTILLES

LESSER ANTILLES

WINDWARD ISLANDS

LEEWARD ISLANDS

Aruba (Neth.)
Curaçao (Neth.)
Bonaire (Neth.)
Willemstad

HONDURAS
Tegucigalpa

NICARAGUA
Managua
León

COSTA RICA
San José
Puerto Limón

PANAMA
CANAL ZONE
Colón
Panamá

COLOMBIA
BARRANQUILLA
Cartagena
Santa Marta

VENEZUELA
MARACAIBO
CARACAS
Valencia
Barquisimeto
Barcelona
Cumaná
Maturín
Ciudad Bolívar
Ciudad Guayana

Port of Spain
TRINIDAD
Tobago

PACIFIC OCEAN

GUYANA

Orinoco

West from Greenwich

Projection: Bi-polar oblique Conical Orthomorphic

COPYRIGHT GEORGE PHILIP & SON LTD.

1:16 000 000

100   0   100   200   300   400   500 miles
100   0   100   200   300   400   500   600   700   800 km

A T L A N T I C   O C E A N

Equator

Paramaribo
Nieuw Amsterdam
Moengo
Mana
Irocoubo
Innamary
Iourou
St. Laurent
Cayenne
Kaw
Approuague
C. Orange
Oiapoque

FR.
GUIANA
Camopi
Camopi

Tumucumaque
Serra
do Navio
Amapá
Araguari
Ilha de Maracá
C. do Norte

AMAPÁ
Macapá

Meriuma
Jari

Mazagão
I. Grande
de Gurupá
Afuá
Chaves
Souré
Salinópolis
Curuçá
Bragança
Vigia
Igarapé-Açu
Viseu
Estuário do
Rio Amazonas
Ilha Caviana
Ilha Mexiana
C. Maguarinho

Óbidos
Monte Alegre
Prainha
Almeirim
Porto de Móz
Breves
Muaná
Gurupá
Belém (Pará)
Abaetetuba
Acará
Cametá

Santarém
Belterra
Altamira
Baião
Capim
Apeú
Guimarães
São Luís (Maranhão)
Alcântara
B. de São Marcos
Barreirinhas
Tutóia
Luís Correia

Aveiro
Brasília Legal
Tucuruí
Tauá
Turiaçu
Cururupu
Itapecuru-
Mirim
Rosário
Parnaíba
Granja
Caucia
Fortaleza (Ceará)
Maranguape

Itaituba
Iriri
Conceição do
Araguaia
Araguacema
Marabá
Imperatriz
Grajaú
Barra do
Corda
Caxias
Codó
União
Timon
Teresina
Piracuruca
Piripiri
Miguel Alves
Brejo
Coroatá
Bacabal
Ipu
Sobral
Maranguape
Baturité
Quixadá
Quixeramobim
Aracati
Areia Branca
Macau
Rocas
Fernando de Noronha
(Braz.)

P A R Á
Xingu
Tocantins
Araguaia
Tocantinópolis
Porto Franco
Carolina
Loreto
Riachão
Novaiorque
Floriano
Uruçuí
Oeiras
Valença do
Piauí
Amarante
Colinas
MARANHÃO
Barra do
Corda
Mossoró
Limoeiro
do Norte
Caraúbos
RIO GRANDE
DO NORTE
Natal
C. de São Roque
Ceará Mirim
Russas
Senador Pompeu
Crateús
Iguatu
Orós
Sousa
CEARÁ
Nova
Cruz
Canguaretama
Cajazeiras
Patos
Campina Grande
PARAÍBA
João Pessoa
(Paraíba)
Caruaru
RECIFE
(Pernambuco)
Cabedelo
Momanguape

B R A Z I L
Sa. dos Carajás
Sa. do Estrondo
Pedro Afonso
Porto Nacional
Natividade
PIAUÍ
São João
do Piauí
Sta. Filomena
Paulistana
Chap. do Araripe
Crato
Juàzeiro do Norte
Pesqueira
Garanhuns
PERNAMBUCO
Viçosa
Palmares
Rio Largo
Barreiros
Ponta de Santo Antão

Iriri
Conceição do
Araguaia
Araguacema
Sa. do Caetité
GOIÁS
Manuel Alves
Peixe
Paranã
Palma
Campos Belos
São Domingos
Sta. Maria
da Vitória
Carinhanha
Sta. Isabel
Ilha do Bananal
Natividade
Taguatinga
Barreiras
Bom Jesus
Serra
da Lapa
Paratinga
Sincorá
BAHIA
Sta. Filomena
Sta. Maria
Caracol
Casa Nova
Remanso
Juàzeiro
Petrolina
Paulo Afonso
Senhor do
Bonfim
Campo
Formoso
Xique-Xique
Barra
Parnaguá
Mundo
Novo
Jacobina
Serrinha
Feira de
Santana
Alagoinhas
São Cristóvão
Aracajú
SERGIPE
Própriá
Penedo
Pal. dos Índios
Maceió
ALAGOAS
Queimadas
Itapicurú
Capelo
São Francisco
Itabuna
Estância

M A T O
G R O S S O
Serra do Roncador
Planalto do
Mato Grosso
Mortes
Aruanã
Uruaçu
1678
Niquelândia
Posse
Corumbaíba
Carinhanha
Coetité
Ituaçu
Brumado
Condeúba
Gavião
Jequié
Vitória da
Conquista
Itabuna
Ilhéus
Canavieiras
Ubaitaba
Itacaré
Belmonte
Porto Seguro

Randonópolis
Baliza
Aragarças
Goiás
Anápolis
Corumbá
DIST.
FED.
Brasília
Formoso
Fluminense
São Francisco
Januária
Monte Azul
Salinas
Pedra Azul
Jequitinhonha
Prado
Caravelas
Banka
Abrolhos
Mucuri
Nanuque

Alto
Araguaia
Jataí
Rio Verde
Morrinhos
Itumbiara
Goiânia
Vianópolis
Ituiutaba
Patrocínio
Paracatú
Bocaiuva
Araçuaí
Teófilo Otoni
Nova
Venécia
Conceição da Barra
São Mateus

Coxim
Baús
Aporé
Catalão
Patos de
Minas
Curvelo
1340
Diamantina
Gov. Valadares
Aimorés

Campo Grande
Agua Clara
Três Lagoas
Nova Granada
Araguari
Uberlândia
Prata
Araxá
Formiga
M I N A S   G E R A I S
Sete
Lagoas
Sabará
Belo Horizonte
Caratinga
Man-
huaçu
Vitória
Pico da
Bandeira
Trindade
(Braz.)

Pres.
Epitácio
Andradina
Panorama
S. José do
Rio Preto
Ribeirão Prêto
Franca
Poços de
Caldas
Lavras
São João del Rei
Barbacena
Juiz de Fora
Campos
Cachoeira de Itapemirim

Pres.
Prudente
Marília
Bauru
Jaú
Piracicaba
Limeira
SÃO
PAULO
Mogí Mirim
Campinas
Petrópolis
RIO DE JANEIRO
Niterói
Cabo Frio

Ponta Pora
Dourados
Assis
Botucatu
Sorocaba
Santos
São Vicente
GUANABARA

COPYRIGHT. GEORGE PHILIP & SON, LTD.

1:16 000 000

100 50 0   100   200   300 miles

100   0   100   200   300   400
km

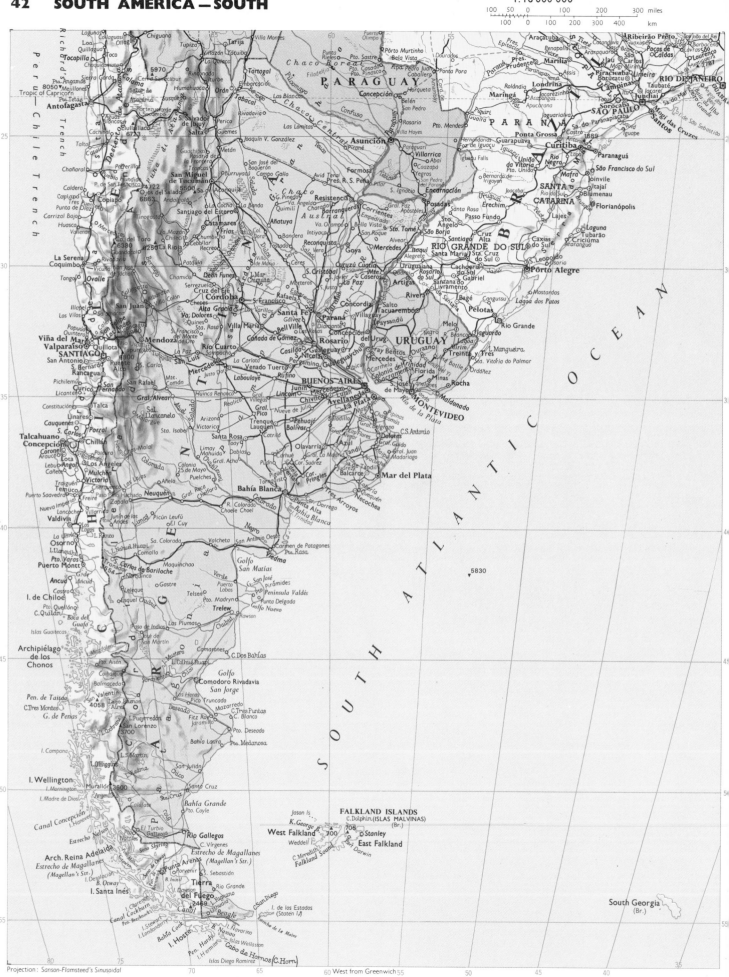

P E R U - C H I L E   T R E N C H

S O U T H   A T L A N T I C   O C E A N

PARAGUAY

Chaco Boreal

Chaco Central

Asunción

Villarrica

Formosa

Resistencia

Corrientes

Posadas

Encarnación

RIO GRANDE DO SUL

URUGUAY

PARANÁ

SANTA CATARINA

SÃO PAULO

RIO DE JANEIRO

Curitiba

Pôrto Alegre

MONTEVIDEO

BUENOS AIRES

La Plata

Mar del Plata

Bahía Blanca

Santiago

Valparaíso

Viña del Mar

Mendoza

Córdoba

Rosario

Santa Fe

Paraná

San Miguel de Tucumán

Salta

Antofagasta

Tropic of Capricorn

La Serena

Coquimbo

Talcahuano

Concepción

Valdivia

Osorno

Puerto Montt

I. de Chiloé

Archipiélago de los Chonos

Comodoro Rivadavia

San Jorge

Golfo San Jorge

Golfo San Matías

Península Valdés

Golfo Nuevo

Trelew

Rawson

Pta. Rasa

Vedma

Neuquén

Río Gallegos

Punta Arenas

Tierra del Fuego

Estrecho de Magallanes (Magellan's Str.)

Cabo de Hornos (C. Horn)

FALKLAND ISLANDS (ISLAS MALVINAS) (Br.)

West Falkland   East Falkland

Stanley

South Georgia (Br.)

A R G E N T I N A

P A T A G O N I A

P A M P A

C H I L E

5830

INDEX

ABBREVIATIONS

Afghan. – *Afghanistan*
Afr. – *Africa*
Alas. – *Alaska*
Alg. – *Algeria*
Amer. – *America*
Ang. – *Angola*
Ant. – *Antarctica*
Arch. – *Archipelago*
Arg. – *Argentina*
Austral. – *Australia*
B. – *Bay, Bight (Baie, Bahia, Baia)*
Belg. – *Belgium*
Br., Brit. – *British, Britain*
Braz. – *Brazil*
C. – *Cape, (Cabo), Coast*
Can. – *Canada*
Cz. – *Czechoslovakia*
Den. – *Denmark*
Des. – *Desert*
Dist. – *District*
E. – *East*
Eng. – *England*
Fin. – *Finland*
Fr. – *France*
G. – *Gulf*
Ger. – *Germany*
Gr. – *Greece*
Gt. – *Great*
Hung. – *Hungary*
I.(s). – *Island)s((Isle, Ile)*
Indon. – *Indonesia*
Ire. – *Ireland*
It. – *Italy*
L. – *Lake, Lough, Loch, Lago*
Mex. – *Mexico*
Mor. – *Morocco*
Moz. – *Mozambique*
Mts. – *Mountains*
N. – *North, Northern*
Neth. – *Netherlands*
Nor. – *Norway*
N.Z. – *New Zealand*
Oc. – *Ocean*
Pac. – *Pacific*
Pen. – *Peninsula*
Phil. – *Philippines*
Pol. – *Poland*
Port. – *Portugal*
Pt. – *Point, Port*
R. – *River, Rio*
Reg. – *Region*
Rep. – *Republic*
Rum. – *Rumania*
S. – *Sea, South*
S. Afr. – *Rep. of South Africa*
Scot. – *Scotland*
st. – *state*
St. – *Saint*
Str. – *Strait*
Swed. – *Sweden*
Switz. – *Switzerland*
Terr. – *Territory*
Turk. – *Turkey*
U.K. – *United Kingdom*
U.S.A. – *United States of America*
U.S.S.R. – *Union of Soviet Socialist Republics*
Ven. – *Venezuela*
W. – *West*
Y-slav. – *Yugoslavia*

The bold figure indicates the map page. The latitudes and longitudes are intended primarily as a guide to finding the places on the map and in some cases are only approximate.

Aac **Ciu**

10 Aachen, Germany 50 47N 6 4E
30 Aba, Nigeria 5 10N 7 19E
21 Abadan, Iran 30 22N 48 20E
12 Abbeville, France 50 6N 1 50E
8 Aberdeen, Scotland 57 9N 2 6W
30 Abidjan, Ivory Coast 5 16N 3 58W
38 Acapulco 18 51N 99 56W
30 Accra, Ghana 5 35N 0 15W
9 Achill Hd., Ireland 53 59N 10 15W
21 Adana, Turkey 37 0N 35 16E
31 Addis Abeba, Ethiopia 9 2N 38 42E
27 Adelaide, Australia 34 55S 138 32E
21 Aden, South Yemen 12 50N 45 0E
21 Aden, G. of, Asia 12 0N 50 E
14 Adriatic Sea, Europe 43 0N 16 0E
15 Ægean Sea, Europe 37 0N 25 0E
21 Afghanistan, St. Asia 33 0N 65 0E
3 Africa, Continent 10 0N 20 0E
22 Agra, India 27 17N 78 13E
38 Aguascalientes, Mex. 22 0N 102 12W
22 Ahmadabad, India 23 0N 72 40E
12 Ajaccio, Corsica, Fr. 41 55N 8 40E
22 Ajmer, India 26 28N 74 37E
24 Akita, Japan 39 45N 140 0E
37 Akron, U.S.A. 41 7N 81 31W
18 Aktyubinsk, U.S.S.R. 50 20N 57 0E
16 Akureyri, Iceland 65 37N 18 3W
22 Akyab, Burma 20 15N 93 0E
21 Al Basrah, Iraq 30 30N 47 55E
21 Al Kuwayt, Kuwait 29 20N 48 0E
21 Al Madinah, Saudi Arabia 24 35N 39 52E
21 Al Mawsil, Iraq 34 0N 45 0E
39 Alajuela, Costa Rica 10 2N 84 8W
34 Alaska, st. U.S.A. 65 0N 150 0W
34 Alaska, G. of 58 0N 145 0W
13 Albacete, Spain 39 0N 1 50W
15 Albania, Rep., Europe 41 0N 20 0E
26 Albany, Australia 35 1S 117 58E
37 Albany, U.S.A. 42 40N 73 47W
17 Ålborg, Denmark 57 3N 9 52E
36 Albuquerque, U.S.A. 35 0N 106 40W
27 Albury, Australia 36 0S 146 50E
29 Aldabra Is., Indian Ocean 9 22S 46 28E
7 Alderney, I., Br. Isles 49 42N 2 12W
12 Alençon, France 48 27N 0 4E
14 Alessándria, Italy 44 54N 8 37E
16 Ålesund, Norway 62 28N 6 5E
34 Aleutian Is., Pac. Oc. 50 0N 175 0W
31 Alexandria = El Iskandarîya 31 0N 30 0E
30 Alger, Algeria 36 42N 3 8E
30 Algeria, St., N. Africa 32 50N 3 0E
13 Alicante, Spain 38 23N 0 30W
26 Alice Springs, Austral. 23 36S 133 53E
22 Allahabad, India 25 25N 81 58E
37 Allegheny Mts., U.S.A. 38 0N 80 0W
37 Allentown, U.S.A. 40 36N 75 30W
18 Alma Ata, U.S.S.R. 43 20N 76 50E
13 Almeria, Spain 36 52N 2 32W
10 Alps, Mts. Europe 46 30N 8 0E
24 Amagaskai, Japan 34 48N 135 35E
36 Amarillo, U.S.A. 35 14N 101 46W
41 Amazonas R. S. America 2 0S 53 30W
12 Amiens, France 49 54N 2 16E
20 Amirantes, Is., Indian Oc. 6 0S 53 0E
21 Amman, Jordan 32 0N 35 52E
22 Amritsar, India 31 35N 74 57E
10 Amsterdam, Neth. 52 23N 4 54E
34 Amundsen G., Canada 70 30N 123 0W
19 Amur, R., U.S.S.R. 53 30N 122 30E
34 Anchorage, Alaska 61 32N 149 50W
14 Ancona, Italy 43 37N 13 30E
22 Andaman Is., India 12 30N 92 30E
40 Andes Mts., 7 0S 85 0W
13 Andorra, st., Europe 42 30N 1 30E
14 Andria, Italy 41 13N 16 17E
19 Andros I., Bahama Is. 24 30N 78 0W
19 Angarsk, U.S.S.R. 52 30N 104 0E
12 Angers, France 47 30N 0 35W
6 Anglesey, I., Wales 53 17N 4 20W
33 Angola, st., Africa 12 0S 18 0E
12 Angoulême, France 45 39N 0 10E
21 Ankara, Turkey 40 0N 32 54E
30 Annaba, Algeria 36 55N 7 45E
25 Anshan, China 41 10N 123 0E
33 Antananarivo, Madagascar 18 55S 47 35E
39 Antigua, I., W. Indies 17 0N 61 50W
42 Antofagasta, Chile 23 50S 70 20W
9 Antrim, N. Ireland 54 40N 6 20W
25 Antung, China 40 10N 124 20E
10 Antwerpen, Belgium 51 13N 4 25E
24 Aomori, Japan 40 45N 140 45E
37 Appalachian Ra., U.S.A. 38 0N 80 0W
20 Arabian Sea, Asia 21 0N 63 0E
41 Aracajú, Brazil 11 0S 37 0W
23 Arafura Sea, E. Indies 10 0S 135 0E
41 Araguaia R., Brazil 7 0S 49 15W
22 Arakan Yoma, Burma 20 0N 94 30E
18 Aral Sea, U.S.S.R. 44 30N 60 0E
18 Aralsk, U.S.S.R. 46 50N 61 20E
8 Arbroath, Scotland 56 34N 2 35W
3 Arctic Ocean, Arctic 78 0N 160 0W
10 Ardennes, Belgium 49 50N 5 10E
39 Arecibo, Puerto Rico 18 29N 66 42W
17 Arendal, Norway 58 28N 8 46E
40 Arequipa, Peru 16 20S 71 30W
14 Arezzo, Italy 43 28N 11 50E
42 Argentina St., S. America 35 0S 60 0W
17 Arhus, Denmark 56 7N 10 11E
18 Arkhangelsk, U.S.S.R. 64 40N 41 0E
9 Arklow, Ireland 52 48N 6 10W
9 Armagh, N. Ireland 54 22N 6 40W
18 Armavir, U.S.S.R. 45 2N 41 7E
27 Armidale, Australia 30 36S 151 40E
10 Arnhem, Neth. 51 58N 5 55E
26 Arnhem Land, Australia 13 10S 135 0E
8 Arran, I., Scotland 55 34N 5 12W
12 Arras, France 50 17N 2 46E
17 Arvika, Sweden 59 42N 68 30E
29 Ascension, I., Atlantic Ocean 8 0S 14 15W
14 Ascoli Piceno, Italy 42 51N 13 34E
28 Ashburton, N.Z. 43 53S 171 48E
7 Ashford, England 51 8N 0 53E
18 Ashkhabad, U.S.S.R. 38 0N 57 50E
4 Asia, Continent 45 0N 75 0E
31 Asmera, Ethiopia 15 19N 38 55E
18 Astrakhan, U.S.S.R. 46 25N 48 5E
42 Asunción, Paraguay 25 11S 57 30W
31 Aswan, Egypt 24 4N 32 57E
31 Asyût, Egypt 27 11N 31 4E
42 Atacama, Desierto de, Chile 24 0S 69 20W
34 Athabasca, L., Canada 59 10N 109 30W
15 Athens = Athînai
15 Athînai, Greece 37 58N 23 46E
9 Athlone, Ireland 53 26N 7 57W
37 Atlanta, U.S.A. 33 50N 84 15W
2 Atlantic Ocean, 0 0 20 0W
28 Auckland, N.Z. 36 52S 174 46E
10 Augsburg, W. Germany 48 22N 10 54E
37 Augusta, U.S.A. 33 29N 81 59W
36 Austin, U.S.A. 30 20N 97 45W
26 Australia, Commonwealth of 10 35S to 43 38S 114 0E to 153 40E
27 Australian Alps, Austral. 36 30S 148 8E
10 Austria, st., Europe 47 0N 14 0E
42 Avellaneda, Argentina 34 50S 58 10W
12 Avignon, France 43 57N 4 50E
7 Avon, Co., England 51 26N 2 35W
7 Avon, R., England 52 8N 1 53W
7 Avonmouth, England 51 30N 2 42W
8 Ayr, Scotland 55 28N 4 37W
2 Azores, Is. Atlantic Oc. 38 44N 29 0W

B

41 Bacabal, Brazil 5 20S 56 45W
23 Bacolod, Philippines, 10 50N 123 0E
13 Badajoz, Spain 38 50N 6 59W
13 Badalona, Spain 41 26N 2 15E
35 Baffin B., Canada 72 0N 65 0W
35 Baffin I., Canada 68 0N 77 0W
21 Baghdad, Iraq 33 20N 44 30E
39 Bahamas, st., W. Indies 24 40N 74 0W
42 Bahía Blanca, Argentina 38 35S 62 13W
21 Bahrain, st., Asia 26 0N 50 35E
27 Bairnsdale, Australia 37 43S 147 35E
36 Bakersfield, U.S.A. 35 25N 119 0W
18 Baku, U.S.S.R. 40 25N 49 45E
13 Baleares, Islas, Spain 39 30N 3 0E
23 Bali, I., Indonesia 8 20S 115 0E
18 Balkhash, L., U.S.S.R. 46 0N 74 50E
27 Ballarat, Australia 37 33S 143 50E
9 Ballymena, N. Ireland 54 53N 6 18W
9 Ballymoney, N. Ireland 55 5N 6 30W
4 Baltic Sea, Europe 56 0N 20 0E
37 Baltimore, U.S.A. 39 18N 76 37W
30 Bamako, Mali 12 48N 7 59W
23 Banda Sea, Indonesia 6 0S 130 0E
23 Bandjarmasin, Indonesia 3 20S 114 25E
9 Bandon, Ireland 51 44N 8 45W
23 Bandung, Indonesia 6 36S 107 48E
39 Banes, Cuba 21 0N 75 42W
8 Banff, Scotland 57 40N 2 32W
22 Bangalore, India 12 59N 77 40E
31 Banghazi, Libya 32 11N 20 3E
23 Bangka, I., Indonesia 2 0S 105 50E
23 Bangkok = Krung Thep
22 Bangladesh, St., Asia 23 40N 90 0E
9 Bangor, N. Ireland 54 40N 5 40W
32 Bangui, Central Africa 4 23N 18 35E
34 Banks I., Canada 73 30N 120 0W
28 Banks Pen. N.Z. 43 45N 173 15E
9 Bantry, Ireland 51 40N 9 28W
39 Barahona, Dominican Rep. 18 13N 71 7W
18 Baranovichi, U.S.S.R. 53 10N 26 0E
39 Barbados, st., W. Indies 13 0N 59 30W
39 Barbuda, I., W. Indies 17 30N 61 40W
27 Barcaldine, Australia 23 33S 145 13E
13 Barcelona, Spain 41 21N 2 10E
22 Bareilly, India 28 22N 79 27E
18 Barents Sea, Arctic Oc. 73 0N 39 0E
14 Bari, Italy 41 6N 16 52E
14 Barletta, Italy 41 20N 16 17E
18 Barnaul, U.S.S.R. 53 20N 83 40E
6 Barnsley, England 53 33N 1 29W
22 Baroda, India 22 20N 73 10E
40 Barquisimeto, Ven. 9 58N 69 13W
8 Barra, I., Scotland 57 0N 7 30W
40 Barranquilla, Colombia 11 0N 74 50W
6 Barrow, England 54 8N 3 15W
10 Basel, Switzerland 47 35N 7 35E
7 Basildon, England 51 34N 0 29E
21 Basra = Al Basrah 30 30N 47 50E
27 Bass Str. Australia 40 0S 146 0E
22 Bassein, Burma 16 0N 94 30E
12 Bastia, Corsica, Fr. 42 40N 9 30E
7 Bath, England 51 22N 2 22W
27 Bathurst, Australia 33 25S 149 31E
37 Baton Rouge, U.S.A. 30 30N 91 5W
18 Batumi, U.S.S.R. 41 30N 41 30E
41 Bauru, Brazil 22 10S 49 0W
37 Bay City, U.S.A. 43 35N 83 51W
12 Bayeux, France 49 17N 0 42W
19 Baykal, L., U.S.S.R. 53 0N 108 0E
12 Bayonne, France 43 30N 1 28W
2 Beaufort Sea, 70 30N 146 0W
33 Beaufort West, S. Africa 32 18S 22 36E
37 Beaumont, U.S.A. 30 5N 94 8W
7 Bedford, & Co., England 52 8N 0 29W
33 Beira, Mozambique 19 50S 34 52E
21 Beirut, Lebanon 33 53N 35 31E
41 Belém, Brazil 1 20S 48 30W
9 Belfast, N. Ireland 54 35N 5 36W
12 Belfort, France 47 38N 6 50E
10 Belgium, King. Europe 51 30N 5 0E
18 Belgorod, U.S.S.R. 50 35N 36 35E
15 Belgrade = Beograd 44 50N 20 37E
38 Belize City, Bleize 17 25N 88 0W
38 Belize, st., Central America 17 0N 88 30W
2 Bellingshausen Sea, Antarctica 66 0S 80 0W
40 Bello, Colombia 6 20N 75 33W
41 Belo Horizonte, Brazil 20 0S 44 0W
8 Ben Nevis, Mt., Scot. 56 48N 5 0W
8 Benbecula, I., Scotland 57 26N 7 20W
27 Bendigo, Australia 36 40S 144 15E
22 Bengal, Gulf of, Asia 17 0N 89 0E
31 Benghazi = Banghazi 32 11N 20 3E
33 Benguela, Angola 12 37S 13 25E
30 Benin, st. (Dahomey) W. Africa 10 0N 2 0E
30 Benin City, Nigeria 6 20N 5 31E
33 Benoni, S. Africa 26 11S 28 18E
15 Beograd, (Belgrade) Yugoslavia 44 50N 20 37E
29 Berbera, Somali Rep. 10 30N 45 2E
18 Berezniki, U.S.S.R. 59 25N 56 5E
14 Bergamo, Italy 45 42N 9 40E
17 Bergen, Norwya 60 23N 5 27E
19 Bering Sea, U.S.S.R. 580N 167 0E
34 Bering Str. U.S.A./U.S.S.R. 66 0N 170 W
36 Berkeley, U.S.A. 38 0N 122 20W
7 Berkshire, Co., England 51 25N 1 0W
10 Berlin, Germany 52 32N 13 24E
10 Bern, Switzerland 46 57N 7 28E
6 Berwick-u.-Tweed, Eng. 55 47N 2 0W
12 Besançon, France 47 15N 6 0E
12 Béziers, France 43 20N 3 12E
22 Bhutan, St., Asia 27 25N 89 50E
11 Białystok, Poland 53 10N 23 10E
12 Biarritz, France 43 29N 1 33W
13 Bilbao, Spain 43 16N 2 56W
36 Billings, U.S.A. 45 43N 108 29W
6 Birkenhead, England 53 24N 3 1W
7 Birmingham, England 52 30N 1 55W
37 Birmingham, U.S.A. 33 40N 86 50W
9 Birr, Ireland 53 7N 7 55W
4 Biscay, B., Atlantic Oc. 45 0N 2 0W
15 Bitola, Yugoslavia 41 5N 21 21E
18 Biysk, U.S.S.R. 52 40N 85 0E
4 Black Sea, Europe 43 30N 35 0E
6 Blackburn, England 53 44N 2 30W
6 Blackpool, England 53 48N 3 3W
12 Blanc, Mont, France-Italy 45 48N 6 50E
33 Blantyre, Malawi 15 45S 35 0E
28 Blenheim, N.Z. 41 38S 174 5E
33 Bloemfontein, S. Africa 29 6S 26 14E
28 Bluff, N.Z. 46 37S 168 20E
30 Bobo Dioulasso, Upper Volta 11 8N 4 13W
16 Boden, Sweden 65 50N 21 42E
16 Bodø, Norway 67 17N 14 27E
40 Bogotá, Colombia 4 34N 74 0W
40 Bolivia, St., S. America 17 6S 64 0W
14 Bologna, Italy 44 30N 11 20E
6 Bolton, England 53 35N 2 26W
14 Bolzano, Italy 46 30N 11 20E
22 Bombay, India 18 55N 72 50E
32 Boma, Zaïre 5 50S 13 4E
35 Bonavista, Canada 48 40N 53 5W
10 Bonn, W. Germany 50 43N 7 6E
6 Bootle, England 53 28N 3 1W
17 Borås, Sweden 57 42N 13 1E
12 Bordeaux, France 44 50N 0 36W
8 Borders, Co. Scotland 55 30N 3 0W
17 Borlange, Sweden 60 28N 15 25E
23 Borneo, I. E. Indies 1 0N 115 0E
17 Bornholm, I., Denmark 55 8N 14 55E
15 Bosna, R., Yugoslavia 44 50N 18 10E
37 Boston, U.S.A. 42 20N 71 0W
16 Bothnia, G. of, Europe 63 0N 21 0E
33 Botswana, st. Africa 23 0S 24 0E
42 Botucatu, Brazil 22 55S 48 30W
30 Bouaké, Ivory Coast 7 40N 4 55W
12 Boulogne, France 50 42N 1 36E
12 Bourges, France 47 5N 2 22E
27 Bourke, Australia 30 8S 145 55E
7 Bournemouth, England 50 43N 1 53W
27 Bowen, Australia 20 0S 148 16E
9 Boyle, Ireland 53 58N 8 19W
6 Bradford, England 53 47N 1 45W
13 Braga, Portugal 41 35N 8 32W
22 Brahmaputra, R., India 26 30N 93 30E
34 Brandon, Canada 49 50N 100 0W
35 Brantford, Canada 43 15N 80 15W
41 Brasília, Brazil 15 30S 47 30W
11 Brasov, Rumania 45 7N 25 39E
10 Bratislava, Cz. 48 10N 17 7E
10 Braunschweig, W.Ger. 52 17N 10 28E
41 Brazil, St., S. America 5 0N to 34 0S 35 0W to 74 0W
32 Brazzaville, Congo 4 9S 15 12E
10 Bremen, W. Germany 53 4N 8 47E
10 Bremerhaven, W.Ger. 53 34N 8 35E
14 Bréscia, Italy 45 33N 10 13E
12 Brest, France 48 24N 4 31W
37 Bridgeport, U.S.A. 41 12N 73 12W
39 Bridgetown, Barbados 13 0N 59 30W
7 Brighton, England 50 50N 0 9W
15 Bríndisi, Italy 40 39N 17 55E
27 Brisbane, Australia 27 25S 152 54E
7 Bristol, England 51 26N 2 35W
7 Bristol, Chan., U.K. 51 18N 3 30W
2 British Antarctic Terr., Antarctica 67 0S 40 0W
3 British Indian Ocean Terr. Indian Ocean 5 0S 70 0E
10 Brno, Czechoslovakia 49 10N 16 35E
15 Brod, Yugoslavia 41 35N 21 17E
8 Brodick, Scotland 55 34N 5 9W
27 Broken Hill, Australia 31 58S 141 29E
10 Brugge, Belgium 51 13N 3 13E
23 Brunei, st. Asia 4 50N 115 0E
10 Brussel, Belgium 50 51N 4 21E
18 Bryansk, U.S.S.R. 53 15N 34 20E
40 Bucaramanga, Colombia 7 0N 73 0W
11 Bucharest = Bucureşti 44 27N 26 10E
7 Buckinghamshire, Co., England 52 0N 0 59W
11 Bucureşti, Rumania 44 27N 26 10E
11 Budapest, Hungary 47 29N 19 5E
42 Buenos Aires, Arg. 34 30S 58 20W
37 Buffalo, U.S.A. 42 55N 78 50W
33 Bulawayo, Rhodesia 20 7S 28 32E
15 Bulgaria St. Europe 42 35N 34 30E
26 Bunbury, Australia 33 20S 115 35E
27 Bundaberg, Australia 24 54S 152 22E
9 Bundoran, Ireland 54 24N 8 17W
24 Bungō-Suidō, Japan 33 0N 132 15E
31 Bûr Said, Egypt 31 16N 32 18E
31 Bûr Sûdan, Egypt 19 32N 37 9E
15 Burgas, Bulgaria 42 33N 27 29E
13 Burgos, Spain 42 21N 3 42W
22 Burma, St., Asia 21 0N 96 30E
27 Burnie, Australia 41 4S 145 56E
6 Burnley, England 53 47N 2 15W
21 Bursa, Turkey 40 15N 29 5E
6 Burton-on-Trent, England 52 48N 1 39W
32 Burundi, st., Africa 3 0S 30 0E
6 Bury, England 53 47N 2 15W
21 Bushehr, Iran 28 55N 50 55E
36 Butte, U.S.A. 46 0N 112 31W
11 Bydgoszcz, Poland 53 10N 18 0E

C

32 Cabinda, Reg., Angola 5 40S 12 11E
13 Cáceres, Spain 39 26N 6 23W
13 Cádiz, Spain 36 30N 6 20W
12 Caen, France 49 10N 0 22W
6 Caernarfon, Wales 53 8N 4 17W
14 Cágliari, Sardinia, Italy 39 15N 9 6E
39 Caguas, Puerto Rico 18 14N 66 4W
39 Caicos Is., W. Indies 21 40N 71 40W
8 Cairngorm, Mts., Scot. 57 6N 3 42W
27 Cairns, Australia 16 55S 145 51E
31 Cairo = El Qahira 30 1N 31 14E
12 Calais, France 50 57N 1 56E
22 Calcutta, India 22 36N 88 24E
34 Calgary, Canada 51 0N 114 10W
40 Cali, Colombia 3 25N 76 35W
22 Calicut, India 11 15N 75 43E
38 California, G. of, Mex. 27 0N 111 0W
40 Callao, Peru 12 0S 77 0W
14 Caltanissetta, Sicily, Italy 37 30N 14 3E
39 Camagüey, Cuba 21 20N 78 0W
23 Cambodia 13 0N 105 0E
7 Camborne, England 50 13N 5 18W
7 Cambrian, Mts., Wales 52 10N 3 52W
7 Cambridge, & Co., Eng. 52 13N 0 8E
32 Cameroon, st., Africa 5 0N 12 30E
38 Campeche, B. de, Mex. 19 30N 93 0W
41 Campina Grande, Brazil 17 20S 35 37W
42 Campinas, Brazil 22 50S 47 0W
41 Campo Grande, Brazil 20 25S 54 40W
41 Campos, Brazil 21 50S 41 20W
34 Canada, st., N.America 60 0N 100 0W
38 Canal Zone, Panama 9 0N 79 45W
30 Canary Is. (Canarias Isles) Atlantic Oc. 29 30N 17 0W
27 Canberra, Australia 35 15S 149 8E
12 Cannes, France 43 32N 7 0E
7 Canterbury, England 51 17N 1 5E
28 Canterbury Bight, N.Z. 44 16S 171 55E
28 Canterbury Plains, N.Z. 43 55S 171 22E
37 Canton, China 23 15N 113 15E
39 Cap Haïtien, Haiti 19 40N 72 20W
35 Cape Breton I., Canada 46 0N 61 0W
33 Cape Town, S. Africa 33 56S 18 28E
2 Cape Verde Is., Atlantic Oc. 17 10N 25 20W
27 Cape York Pen. Australia 13 30S 142 30E
40 Caracas, Venezuela 10 30N 66 50W
7 Cardiff, Wales 51 28N 3 11W
7 Cardigan, B., Wales 52 30N 4 30W
39 Caribbean Sea, W. Indies 15 0N 75 0W
6 Carlisle, England 54 54N 2 55W
9 Carlow, & Co., Ireland 52 50N 6 58W
7 Carmarthen, Wales 51 56N 4 8W
26 Carnarvon, Australia 24 51S 113 42E
3 Caroline Is., Pacific Oc. 8 0N 150 0E
11 Carpathians, Mts. Europe 46 20N 26 0E
27 Carpentaria, G. of, Austral. 14 0S 139 0E
13 Cartagena, Colombia 10 20N 75 30W
40 Cartagena, Spain 37 38N 0 59W
41 Caruaru, Brazil 8 15S 35 55W
40 Carúpano, Venezuela 10 45N 63 15W
30 Casablanca, Morocco 33 30N 7 37W
36 Casper, U.S.A. 42 52N 106 27W
18 Caspian Sea, U.S.S.R. 43 0N 50 0E
13 Castellón de la Plana, Spain 39 58N 0 3W
9 Castlebar, Ireland 53 52N 9 20W
9 Castlereagh, Ireland 53 47N 8 30W
39 Castries, W. Indies 14 0N 60 50W
14 Catánia, Sicily, Italy 37 31N 15 4E
14 Catanzaro, Italy 38 53N 16 36E
9 Cavan & Co., Ireland 54 0N 7 22W
41 Cayenne, Fr. Guiana 5 0N 52 18W
39 Cayman Is., W. Indies 19 40N 79 50W
23 Cebu, Philippes 10 30N 124 0E
37 Cedar Rapids, U.S.A. 42 0N 91 38W
23 Celebes, I. (Sulawesi) Indonesia 2 0S 120 0E
23 Celebes Sea, Asia 3 0N 123 0E
8 Central, Co. Scotland 56 20N 4 20W
32 Central Africa, st., Africa 7 0N 20 0E
23 Ceram Sea, Indonesia 2 30S 128 30E
30 Ceuta, Morocco 25 52N 5 26W
22 Ceylon = Sri Lanka
31 Chad. st., Africa 12 0N 17 0E
3 Chagos Arch., Indian Oc. 6 0S 72 0E
12 Châlon, France 46 48N 4 50E
12 Châlons, France, 48 48N 4 20E
12 Chambéry, France 45 34N 5 55E
25 Changchow, China 31 45N 120 0E
25 Changchun, China 43 58N 125 9E
25 Changkiakow, China 40 52N 114 45E
25 Changkiang, China 21 7N 110 21E
25 Changsha, China 28 5N 113 1E
7 Channel Is., British Is. 49 30N 2 40W
37 Charleston, U.S.A. 32 55N 80 0W
27 Charleville, Australia 26 24S 146 15E
37 Charlotte, U.S.A. 35 16N 80 46W
37 Charlottesville, U.S.A. 38 1N 78 30W
35 Charlottetown, Canada 46 19N 63 3W
27 Charters Towers, Australia 20 5S 146 13E
12 Chartres, France 48 29N 1 30E
35 Chatham, Canada 47 2N 65 28W
37 Chattanooga, U.S.A. 35 0N 85 20W
18 Cheboksary, U.S.S.R. 56 8N 47 30E
7 Chelmsford, England 51 44N 0 29E
7 Cheltenham, England 51 53N 2 7W
18 Chelyabinsk, U.S.S.R. 55 10N 61 35E
25 Chengchow, China 34 45N 113 45E
25 Chengtu, China 30 40N 104 12E
12 Cherbourg, France 49 39N 1 40W
18 Cherepovets, U.S.S.R. 59 5N 37 55E
18 Chernigov, U.S.S.R. 51 28N 31 20E
18 Chernovtsy, U.S.S.R. 48 0N 26 0E
7 Cherwell, R., England 51 56N 1 18W
37 Chesapeake B., U.S.A. 38 0N 76 12W
6 Cheshire, Co., England 53 14N 2 30W
6 Chester, England 53 12N 2 53W
6 Chesterfield, England 53 14N 1 26W
36 Cheyenne, U.S.A. 41 9N 104 49W
24 Chiba, Japan 35 30N 140 7E
37 Chicago, U.S.A. 41 56N 87 50W
40 Chidayo, Peru 6 42S 79 50W
35 Chicoutimi, Canada 48 28N 71 5W
38 Chihuahua, Mexico 28 40N 106 3W
42 Chile St., S. America 17 30S to 55 0S 71 15W
42 Chillán, Chile 36 40S 72 10W
7 Chiltern Hills, England 51 44N 0 42W
40 Chimbote, Peru 9 0S 78 35W
18 Chimkent, U.S.S.R. 42 40N 69 25E
25 China, st., Asia 55 0N to 18 30W 70 0E to 133 0E
39 Chinandego, Nicaragua 12 30N 87 0W
25 Chinchow, China 41 10N 121 10E
19 Chita, U.S.S.R. 52 0N 113 25E
22 Chittagong, Bangladesh 22 19N 91 55E
25 Chongjin, N. Korea 41 40N 129 40E
11 Chorzów, Poland 50 18N 19 0E
28 Christchurch, N.Z. 43 33S 172 39E
24 Chūgaku-Sanchi, Japan 35 0N 133 0E
25 Chungking, China 29 35N 106 50E
34 Churchill, Canada 58 45N 94 5W
39 Ciego de Avila, Cuba 21 50N 78 50W
39 Cienfuegos, Cuba 22 10N 80 30W
37 Cincinnati, U.S.A. 39 8N 84 25W
38 Ciudad Acuña, Mex. 29 20N 101 10W
38 Ciudad Juárez, Mex. 31 40N 106 28W
38 Ciudad Madero, Mex. 22 19N 97 50W

38 Ciudad Obregón, Mexico 27 28N 109 59W
13 Ciudad Real, Spain 38 59N 3 55W
38 Ciudad Victoria, Mex. 23 41N 99 9W
9 Clare, Co., Ireland 52 52N 8 35W
9 Claremorris, Ireland 53 45N 9 0W
27 Clermont, Australia 22 46S 147 38E
12 Clermont Ferrand, France 45 46N 3 4E
37 Cleveland, U.S.A. 41 28N 81 43W
6 Cleveland, Co., England 54 35N 1 20W
27 Cloncurry, Australia 20 40S 140 28E
9 Clones, Ireland 54 10N 7 13W
11 Cluj, Rumania 46 47N 23 38E
6 Clwyd, Co., Wales 53 10N 3 30W
8 Clyde, Firth of, Scotland 55 20N 5 0W
8 Clyde, R., Scotland 55 46N 3 58W
8 Clydebank, Scotland 55 54N 4 25W
36 Coast Ra., N. America 40 0N 124 0W
8 Coatbridge, Scotland 55 52N 4 2W
38 Coatzacoalcos, Mexico 18 7N 94 35W
35 Cobalt, Canada 47 25N 79 42W
9 Cobh, Ireland 51 50N 8 18W
40 Cochabamba, Bolivia 17 15S 66 20W
35 Cochrane, Canada 49 0N 81 0W
3 Cocos Is., Indian Oc. 12 12S 96 54E
22 Coimbatore, India 11 2N 76 59E
13 Coimbra, Portugal 40 15N 8 27W
7 Colchester, England 51 54N
9 Coleraine, N. Ireland 55 8N 6 40E
38 Colima, Mexico 19 10N 103 40W
8 Coll, I., Scotland 56 40N 6 3W
9 Collooney, Ireland 54 11N 8 28W
10 Cologne=Köln, W.Ger. 50 56N 8 58E
40 Colombia, St., S. America 3 45N 73 0W
22 Colombo, Sri Lanka 6 56N 79 58E
38 Colon, Panama 9 20N 80 0W
8 Colonsay, I., Scotland 56 4N 6 12W
36 Colorado, R., U.S.A. 33 30N 114 30W
36 Colorado Springs, U.S.A. 38 50N 104 50W
37 Columbia, U.S.A. 34 0N 81 0W
36 Columbia, R., U.S.A. 51 50N 118 0W
37 Columbus, Ga., U.S.A. 32 30N 84 58W
37 Columbus, Ohio, U.S.A. 39 57N 83 1W
6 Colwyn Bay, Wales 53 17N 3 44W
14 Como, Italy 45 48N 9 5E
30 Conakry, Guinea 9 29N 13 49W
42 Concepción, Chile 36 50S 73 0W
42 Concepción, Paraguay 23 30S 57 20W
42 Concordia, Argentina 31 20S 58 2W
32 Congo, R., Africa 2 0N 23 0E
32 Congo, st., Africa 2 0S 16 0E
11 Constanţa, Rumania 44 14N 28 38E
30 Constantine, Algeria 36 25N 6 30E
28 Cook Is., Pacific Oc. 22 0S 157 0W
28 Cook, Mt., N.Z. 43 36S 170 9E
28 Cook Str., N.Z. 41 15S 174 29E
27 Cooktown, Australia 15 30S 145 16E
26 Coolgardie, Australia 30 55S 121 8E
17 Copenhagen = København
27 Coarl Sea Is., Terr., 20 0S 155 0E
42 Córdoba, Argentina 31 20S 64 10W
13 Córdoba, Spain 37 50N 4 50W
15 Corfu = Kérkira, I.
9 Cork, & Co., Ireland 51 54N 8 30W
35 Corner Brook, Canada 49 0N 58 0W
7 Cornwall, Co., England 50 26N 4 40W
36 Corpus Christi, U.S.A. 27 50N 97 28W
42 Corrientes, Argentina 27 30S 58 45W
12 Corsica, I. Mediterranean Sea 42 0N 9 0E
14 Cosenza, Italy 39 17N 16 14E
39 Costa Rica st., Central America 10 0N 84 0W
30 Cotonou, Benin 6 20N 2 25E
7 Cotswold Hills, England 51 42N 2 10W
7 Coventry, England 52 25N 1 31W
27 Cowra, Australia 33 49S 148 42E
11 Craiova, Rumania 44 21N 23 48E
14 Cremona, Italy 45 8N 10 2E
15 Crete = Kriti, I. 35 20N 25 0E
6 Crewe, England 53 6N 2 28W
39 Cuba, st., W. Indies 22 0N 79 0W
40 Cúcuta, Colombia 8 0N 72 30W
40 Cuenca, Ecuador 2 50S 79 9W
13 Cuenca, Spain 45 0N 2 10W
41 Cuiabá, Brazil 15 30S 56 0W
38 Culiacan, Mexico 24 50N 107 40W
6 Cumbria, Co., England 54 30N 3 0W
6 Cumbrian, Mts., Eng. 54 30N 3 0W
27 Cunnamulla, Australia 28 2S 145 38E
40 Curaçao, Neth. W. Indies 12 10N 69 0W
40 Curaray, R., Peru 1 30S 75 30W
42 Curitiba, Brazil 25 20S 49 10W
21 Cyprus, st., Medit. Sea 35 0N 33 0E
10 Czechoslovakia, st. Europe 49 0N 17 0E
11 Czestochowa, Poland 50 49N 19 7E

D

23 Da Nang, Vietnam 16 10N 108 7E
22 Dacca, Bangladesh 23 43N 90 26E
30 Dahomey = Benin
30 Dakar, Senegal 14 34N 17 29W
27 Dalby, Australia 27 10S 151 17E
37 Dallas, U.S.A. 32 50N 96 50W
21 Damascus = Dimashq
26 Dampier, Australia 20 40S 116 30E
28 Dannevirke, N.Z. 40 12S 176 8E
11 Danube, R., Europe 45 0N 28 20E
32 Dar-es-Salaam, Tanzania 6 50S 39 12E
28 Dargaville, N.Z. 35 57S 173 52E
40 Darien, G. del, Colombia 9 0N 77 0W
27 Darling, R., Austral. 31 0S 144 30E
26 Darling Ra., Australia 32 30S 116 0E
6 Darlington, England 54 33N 1 33W
7 Dartmoor, England 50 36N 4 0W
35 Dartmouth, Canada 44 40N 63 30W
26 Darwin, Austral. 12 20S 130 50E
18 Daugavpils, U.S.S.R. 55 53N 26 32E
34 Dauphin, Canada 51 15N 100 5W
23 Davao, Philippines 7 0N 125 40E
39 David, Panama 8 30N 82 30W
35 Davis Str., N. America 66 30N 59 0W
34 Dawson, Canada 64 10N 139 30W
34 Dawson Creek, Can. 55 45N 120 15W
37 Dayton, U.S.A. 39 45N 84 10W
11 Debrecen, Hungary 47 33N 21 42E
8 Dee, R., Scotland 57 4N 3 7W
22 Delhi, India 28 38N 77 17E
17 Denmark, st., Europe 55 30N 9 0E
2 Denmark Str., Atlantic Oc. 66 0N 30 0W
36 Denver, U.S.A. 39 48N 105 0W
26 Derby, Australia 17 18S 123 40E
6 Derby & Co., England 52 55N 1 28W
37 Des Moines, U.S.A. 41 29N 93 40W
37 Detroit, U.S.A. 42 20N 83 5W
7 Devon, Co., England 50 45N 3 45W
28 Devonport, N.Z. 36 49S 174 49E
6 Dewsbury, England 53 42N 1 38W
33 Diego-Suarez, Madagascar 12 25S 49 20E
12 Dieppe, France 49 54N 1 4E
12 Dijon, France 47 20N 5 0E
21 Dimashq (Damasus) Syria 33 30N 36 18E
8 Dingwall, Scotland 57 36N 4 26W
23 Djakarta, Indonesia 6 9S 106 49E
29 Djibouti, st., Africa 11 30N 43 3E
18 Dnepropetrovsk, U.S.S.R. 48 30N 35 0E
39 Dominica, I., Winward Is. 15 20N 61 20W
39 Dominican Republic, st. W. Indies 19 0N 70 30W
8 Don, R., Scotland 57 14N 2 15W
6 Doncaster, England 53 31N 1 9W
9 Donegal & Co., Ireland 54 39N 8 8W
9 Donegal, B., Ireland 54 30N 8 35W
18 Donetsk, U.S.S.R. 48 7N 37 50E
7 Dorset, Co., England 50 48N 2 25W
10 Dortmund, W. Germany 51 32N 7 28E
12 Douai, France 50 21N 3 4E
32 Douala, Cameroon 4 0N 9 45E
6 Douglas, I. of Man 54 9N 4 29W
13 Douro, R., Portugal 41 1N 8 16W
7 Dover, England 51 7N 1 19E
33 Drakensberg, Mts., S. Africa 31 0S 25 0E
17 Drammen, Norway 59 42N 10 12E
15 Drava, R., Yugoslavia 45 50N 18 0W
10 Dresden, E. Germany 51 2N 13 45E
15 Drina, R., Yugoslavia 44 30N 19 10E
9 Drogheda, Ireland 53 45N 6 20W
34 Drumheller, Canada 51 25N 112 40W
27 Dubbo, Australia 32 11S 148 35E
9 Dublin & Co., Ireland 53 20N 6 18W
15 Dubrovnik, Y-slav. 42 39N 18 6E
10 Duisburg, W. Germany 51 27N 6 42E
37 Duluth, U.S.A. 46 48N 92 10W
8 Dumbarton, Scotland 55 58N 4 35W
8 Dumfries, Scotland 55 12N 3 30W
8 Dumfries & Galloway, Co., Scot. 55 10N 3 50W
9 Dun Lagohaire, lerland 53 17N 6 9W
9 Dundalk, Ireland 53 55N 6 45W
8 Dundee, Scotland 56 29N 3 0W
28 Dunedin, N.Z. 45 50S 170 33E
8 Dunfermline, Scotland 56 5N 3 28W
9 Dungannon, N. Ireland 54 30N 6 47W
9 Dungarvan, Ireland 52 6N 7 40W
12 Dunkerque, France 51 2N 2 20E
8 Dunnet Hd., Scotland 58 38N 3 22W
38 Durango, U.S.A. 37 10N 107 50W
33 Durban, S. Africa 29 49S 31 1E
6 Durham, Co., England 54 42N 1 45W
18 Dushanbe, U.S.S.R. 38 50N 68 50E
10 Düsseldorf, W.Ger. 51 15N 6 46E
7 Dyfed, Co., Wales 52 0N 4 0W
18 Dzerzhinsk, U.S.S.R. 56 15N 43 15E
25 Dzungaria, China 44 10N 88 0E

E

25 East China Sea, Asia 27 0N 125 0E
33 East London, S. Africa 33 0S 27 55E
7 East Sussex, Co., England 51 0N 0 30E
7 Eastbourne, England 50 46N 0 18E
22 Eastern Ghats, India 15 0N 80 0E
13 Ebro, R., Spain 41 49N 1 5W
40 Ecuador, St., S. America 2 0S 79 0W
8 Edinburgh, Scotland 55 57N 3 12W
34 Edmonton, Canada 53 30N 113 30W
35 Edmundston, Canada 47 23N 68 20W
31 Egypt, st., N. Africa 25 0N 30 0E
10 Eindhoven, Netherlands 51 26N 5 30E
31 El Faiyûm, Egypt 29 19N 30 50E
13 El Ferrol, Spain 43 29N 3 14W
31 El Gîza, Egypt 30 0N 31 10E
31 El Iskandarîya, (Alexandria) Egypt 31 0N 30 0E
31 El Khartûm, Sudan 15 31N 32 35E
31 El Marsûra, Egypt 31 0N 31 19E
31 El Minyâ, Egypt 28 7N 30 33E
31 El Obeid, Sudan 13 8N 30 10E
36 El Paso, U.S.A. 31 50N 106 30W
31 El Qâhira (Cairo) Egypt 30 1N 31 14E
31 El Suweis (Suez) Egypt 29 58N 32 31E
14 Elba, I., Italy 42 48N 10 15E
10 Elbe, R. Germany 53 15N 10 7E
18 Elbrus, Mt., U.S.S.R. 43 30N 42 30E
21 Elburz Mts., Iran 36 0N 52 0E
13 Elche, Spain 38 15N 0 42W
8 Elgin, Scotland 57 39N 3 20W
2 Ellesmere I., Canada 79 30N 80 0W
3 Ellice Is. (Tuvalu), Pacific Oc. 8 0S 176 0E
27 Emerald, Australia 23 30S 148 11E
38 Empalme, Mexico 28 1N 110 49W
3 Enderby Land, Antarctica 66 0S 53 0E
18 Engels, U.S.S.R. 51 28N 46 6E
6 England, U.K. 50 to 55 45N 1 40E to 5 40W
7 English Chan., Europe 50 0N 2 0W
9 Ennis, Ireland 52 51N 8 59W
9 Enniskillen, N. Ireland 52 30N 6 35W
32 Entebbe, Uganda 0 3N 32 30E
30 Enugu, Nigeria 6 30N 7 30E
32 Equatorial Guinea, st., Africa 2 0N 10 E
37 Erie, U.S.A. 42 7N 80 2W
37 Erie, L., N. America 42 30N 82 0W
31 Eritrea, Reg., Ethiopia 14 0N 41 0E
9 Erne, L., N. Ireland 54 14N 7 30W
21 Erzurum, Turkey 39 57N 41 15E
17 Esbjerg, Denmark 55 29N 8 29E
21 Esfahan, Iran 32 43N 51 33E
17 Eskilstuna, Sweden 59 22N 16 32E
26 Esperance, Australia 33 45S 121 55E
40 Essequibo, R., Guyana 5 45N 58 50W
10 Essen, W. Germany 51 28N 6 59E
7 Essex, Co., England 51 48N 0 30E
31 Ethiopia, st., Africa 8 0N 40 0E
14 Etna, Mt., Italy 37 45N 15 0E
36 Eugene, U.S.A. 44 0N 123 8W
21 Euphrates, R., Iraq 33 30N 43 0E
37 Evansville, U.S.A. 38 0N 87 35W
22 Everest, Mt., Nepal 28 5N 86 58E
15 Evvoia, I., Greece 38 30N 24 0E
7 Exeter, England 50 43N 3 31W
27 Eyre, L., Australia 29 0S 137 20E
26 Eyre Pen., Australia 33 30S 137 17E

F

17 Fagersta, Sweden 60 1N 15 46E
34 Fairbanks, Alaska 64 59N 147 40W
8 Falkirk, Scotland 56 0N 3 47W
42 Falkirk Islands, Atlantic Oc. 51 30S 58 30W
2 Falkland Islands Dependencies, Southern Oc. 55 0S 45 0W
17 Falun, Sweden 60 32N 15 39E
7 Fareham, England 50 52N 1 11W
37 Fargo, U.S.A. 47 0N 97 0W
2 Faroe Is., N. Atlantic Oc. 62 0N 7 0W
28 Fielding, N.Z. 40 13S 175 35E
7 Felixtowe, England 51 58N 1 22W
14 Ferrard, Italy 44 50N 11 26E
30 Fés, Morocco 34 5N 4 54W
8 Fife, Co., Scotland 56 13N 3 2W
28 Fiji, Is., Pacific Ocean 17 20S 179 0E
8 Findhorn, R., Scotland 57 30N 3 45W
13 Finisterre, C., Spain 42 50N 9 19W
16 Finland, st., Europe 70 0N 27 0E
14 Firenze, Italy 43 47N 11 15E
7 Fishguard, Wales 51 59N 4 59W
6 Flamborough Hd., Eng. 54 8N 0 4W
10 Flensburg, Germany 54 46N 9 28E
27 Flinders Ra., Australia 31 30S 138 30E
37 Flint, U.S.A. 43 0N 83 40W
23 Flores Sea, Indonesia 6 30S 124 0E
14 Florence = Firenze
42 Florianópolis, Brazil 27 30S 48 30W
37 Florida Str., U.S.A. 25 0N 80 0W
14 Fóggia, Italy 41 28N 15 31E
7 Folkestone, England 51 5N 1 11E
12 Fontainbleau, France 48 24N 2 40E
25 Foochow, China 26 9N 119 25E
25 Formosa = Taiwan
4 Føroyar, Is., Atlantic Oc. 62 0N 7 0W
37 Fort Smith, U.S.A. 35 25N 94 25W
37 Fort Wayne, U.S.A. 41 5N 85 10W
8 Fort William, Scotland 56 48N 5 8W
36 Fort Worth, U.S.A. 32 45N 97 25W
34 Fort Yukon, Alaska 66 35N 145 12W
39 Fort-de-France, Martinique 14 36N 61 2W
41 Fortaleza, Brazil 3 35S 38 35W
8 Forth, Firth of, Scotland 56 5N 2 55W
12 France, st., Europe 47 0N 3 0E
10 Frankfurt, W. Germany 50 7N 8 40E
34 Fraser, R., Canada 53 30N 120 40W
8 Fraserburgh, Scotland 57 41N 2 0W
35 Fredericton, Canada 45 57N 66 40W
17 Frederikshavn, Den. 57 28N 10 31E
17 Fredrikstad, Norway 59 13N 10 57E
39 Freeport, Bahamas 42 18N 89 40W
30 Freetown, Sierra Leone 8 30N 13 10W
10 Freiburg, Germany 48 0N 7 52E
26 Fremantle, Australia 32 1S 115 47E
41 French Guiana, S. America 4 0N 53 0W
38 Fresnillo, Mexico 23 10N 103 0W
36 Fresno, U.S.A. 36 47N 119 50W
18 Frunze, U.S.S.R. 42 40N 74 50E
24 Fukuoka, Japan 33 30N 130 30E
24 Funabashi, Japan 33 45N 140 0E
27 Furneaux Group, Is., Tasmania 40 10S 147 56E
25 Fushun, China 41 55N 123 55E
17 Fyn, I., Denmark 55 18N 10 20E
8 Fyne, L., Denmark 55 20N 10 30E

G

32 Gabon, st., Africa 2 0S 12 0E
15 Gabrovo, Bulgaria 42 52N 25 27E
2 Galapagos Is., Pacific Oc. 0 0 89 0W
11 Galaţi, Rumania 45 27N 28 2E
16 Gällivare, Sweden 67 7N 20 32E
8 Galloway, Mull of, Scot. 54 38N 4 50W
37 Galveston, U.S.A. 29 15N 94 48W
9 Galway & Co., Ireland 53 16N 9 4W
9 Galway, B., Ireland 53 10N 9 20W
30 Gambia, st., W. Africa 13 25N 16 0W
22 Ganga, R., India 25 0N 88 0E
22 Ganges, R. = Ganga R.
14 Garda, L. di, Italy 45 40N 10 40E
12 Garonne, R., France 44 45N 0 32W
35 Gaspé Pen., Canada 48 45N 65 40W
6 Gateshead, England 54 57N 1 37W
17 Gävle, Sweden 60 41N 17 13E
31 Gaza, Egypt 31 30N 34 28E
11 Gdańsk, Poland 54 22N 18 40E
11 Gdyńia, Poland 54 35N 18 33E
27 Geelong, Australia 38 2S 144 20E
10 Genève, Switzerland 46 12N 6 9E
14 Génova (Genoa) Italy 44 24N 8 56E
10 Gent, Belgium 51 2N 3 37E
40 Georgetown, Guyana 6 50N 58 12W
26 Geraldton, Australia 28 48S 114 32E
10 Germany, East, st. Europe 52 0N 12 0E
10 Germany, West, st., Europe 52 0N 9 0E
33 Germiston, S. Africa 26 11S 28 10E
13 Gerona, Spain 41 58N 2 46E
30 Ghana, st., W. Africa 6 0N 1 0W
9 Giant's Causeway, N. Ireland 55 15N 6 30W
13 Gibraltar, Europe 36 7N 5 22W
26 Gibson Desert, Australia 24 0S 125 0E
24 Gifu, Japan 35 30N 136 45E
13 Gijón, Spain 43 32N 5 42W
3 Gilbert Is., Pacific Oc. 1 0S 176 0E
7 Gillingham, England 51 23N 0 34E
8 Girvan, Scotland 55 15N 4 50W
28 Gisborne, N.Z. 38 39S 178 5E
17 Gjøvik, Norway 60 47N 10 43E
35 Glace Bay, Canada 46 11N 59 58W
27 Gladstone, Australia 23 52S 151 16E
17 Glamå, R., Norway 60 30N 12 8E
8 Glasgow, Scotland 55 52N 4 14W
27 Glen Innes, Australia 29 40S 151 39E
36 Glendale, U.S.A. 34 7N 118 18W
7 Gloucester & Co., England 51 52N 2 15W
22 Godavari, R., India 19 5N 79 0E
41 Goiânia, Brazil 16 35S 49 20W
18 Gomel, U.S.S.R. 52 28N 31 0E
38 Gómez Palacio, Mexico 25 40N 104 40W
33 Good Hope, C. of, S. Africa 34 24S 18 30E
28 Gore, N.Z. 46 5S 168 58E
18 Gorkiy, U.S.S.R. 57 20N 44 0E
7 Gosport, England 50 48N 1 8W
17 Göteborg, Sweden 57 43N 11 59E
17 Gotland, I., Swdeen 58 15N 18 30E
27 Goulburn, Australia 32 22S 149 31E
41 Governador Valadares, Brazil 18 15S 41 57W
14 Gozo, I., Malta 36 0N 14 13E
27 Grafton, Australia 29 35S 152 0E
2 Graham Land, Antacrtica 67 0S 65 0W
33 Grahamstown, S. Africa 33 19S 26 31E
8 Grampian, Co., Scot. 57 30N 2 40W
8 Grampian Highlands, Scotland 56 50N 4 0W
39 Granada, Nicaragua 11 58N 86 0W
13 Granada, Spain 37 10N 3 35W
36 Grand Canyon, U.S.A. 36 20N 113 30W
37 Grand Forks, U.S.A. 48 0N 97 3W
37 Grand Rapids, U.S.A. 42 57N 85 40W
34 Grande Prairie, Can. 55 15N 118 50W
10 Graz, Austria 47 4N 15 27E
39 Great Abaco, I. Bahamas 26 30N 77 20W
26 Great Australian Bight, Australia 33 0S 130 0E
27 Great Barrier Reef, Australia 19 0S 149 0E
34 Great Bear L., Canada 65 0N 120 0W
27 Great Divide, Mts., Australia 23 0S 146 0E
36 Great Falls, U.S.A. 47 29N 111 19W
36 Great Salt L. U.S.A. 41 0N 112 30W
26 Great Sandy Desert, Australia 21 0S 124 0E
34 Great Slave L., Can. 61 30N 114 20W
26 Great Victoria Desert, Australia 29 30S 126 30E
6 Great Yarmouth, Eng. 52 40N 1 45E
39 Greater Antilles, W. Indies 17 40N 74 0W
15 Greece, St. Europe 40 0N 23 0E
37 Green Bay, U.S.A. 44 30N 88 0W
35 Greenland, N. America 66 0N 45 0W
8 Greenock, Scotland 55 57N 4 46W
37 Greensboro, U.S.A. 36 5N 79 47W
39 Grenada I., W. Indies 12 10N 61 40W
12 Grenoble, France 45 12N 5 42E
28 Greymouth, N.Z. 42 29S 171 13E
27 Griffith, Australia 34 14S 145 46E
6 Grimsby, England 53 35N 0 5W
18 Grodno, U.S.S.R. 53 42N 23 52E
10 Groningen, Netherlands 53 15N 6 35E
18 Groznyy, U.S.S.R. 43 20N 45 45E
38 Guadalajara, Mexico 20 40N 103 20W
13 Guadalquiver, R., Spain 38 0N 4 0W
39 Guadeloupe, I., Fr. W. Indies 16 20N 61 40W
13 Guadiana, R., Spain 37 55N 7 39W
13 Guadix, Spain 37 18N 3 11W
39 Guanabacoa, Cuba 23 8N 82 18W
39 Guantánamo, Cuba 20 10N 75 20W
42 Guarapuava, Brazil 25 20S 51 30W
38 Guatemala, st. Central America 15 40N 90 30W
38 Guatemala, Guatemala, 14 40N 90 30
40 Guaviare, R., Colombia 3 30N 71 0W
40 Guayaquil, Ecuador 2 15N 79 52W
38 Guaymas, Mexico 27 50N 111 0W
7 Guernsey, I., Brit. Isles 49 30N 2 35W
7 Guildford, England 51 14N 0 34W
30 Guinea, st., W. Africa 10 20N 10 0W
29 Guinea, G. of, W. Africa 3 0N 2 30E
30 Guinea-Bissau, st., W. Africa 12 0N 15 0W
22 Gujranwala, Pakistan 32 10N 74 12E
18 Guryev, U.S.S.R. 47 5N 52 0E
40 Guyana, St., S. America 5 0N 59 0W
22 Gwalior, India 26 12N 78 10E
33 Gwelo, Rhodesia 19 28S 29 45E
7 Gwent, Co., Wales 51 40N 3 0W
6 Gwynedd, Co., Wales 53 0N 4 0N
27 Gympie, Australia 26 11S 152 38E

H

10 Haarlem, Netherlands 52 23N 4 39E
24 Hachiōji, Japan 35 30N 139 30E
21 Haifa, Israel 32 48N 35 0E
39 Haiti, st., W. Indies 19 6N 72 30W
24 Hakodate, Japan 41 45N 140 44E
21 Halab (Aleppo) Syria 36 12N 37 13E
35 Halifax, Canada 44 38N 63 35W
6 Halifax, England 53 43N 1 51W
10 Halle, E. Germany 51 29N 12 0E
23 Halmahera, I., Indonesia 0 40N 128 0E
17 Halmstad, Sweden 56 37N 12 56E
21 Hamá, Syria 35 5N 36 40E
21 Hamadan, Iran 34 52N 48 32E
17 Hamar, Norway 60 48N 11 7E
24 Hamamatsu, Japan 34 45N 137 45E
10 Hamburg W. Germany 53 32N 9 59E
17 Hämeenlinna, Finland 61 3N 24 26E
35 Hamilton, Canada 43 20N 79 50W
28 Hamilton, N.Z. 37 47S 175 19E
8 Hamilton, Scotland 55 47N 4 2W
16 Hammerfest, Norway 70 33N 23 50E
7 Hampshire, Co., England 51 3N 1 20W
25 Hangchow, China 30 20N 120 5E
17 Hangö, Finland 59 59N 22 57E
10 Hannover, W. Germany 52 23N 9 43E
23 Hanoi, Vietnam 21 5N 105 40E
16 Haparanda, Sweden 65 52N 24 8E
25 Harbin, China 45 45N 126 41E
16 Härnösand, Sweden 62 38N 18 5E
8 Harris, Scotland 57 50N 6 55W
37 Harrisburg, U.S.A. 40 18N 76 52W
6 Harrogate, England 53 59N 1 32W
37 Hartford, U.S.A. 41 47N 72 41W
6 Hartlepool, England 54 42N 1 11W
7 Harwich, England 51 56N 1 18E
7 Hastings, England 50 51N 0 36E
28 Hastings, N.Z. 39 39S 176 52E
36 Hawaiian Is., Pacific Oc. 20 0N 155 0W
8 Hawick, Scotland 55 25N 2 48W
27 Hawker, Australia 31 59S 138 22E
35 Hearst, Canada 49 40N 83 41W
10 Heidelberg, W. Ger. 49 23N 8 41E
17 Helsingborg, Sweden 56 3N 12 42E
17 Helsingør, Denmark 56 2N 12 35E
17 Helsinki, Finland 60 15N 25 3E
25 Hengyang, China 26 58N 112 25E
21 Herat, Afghanistan 34 20N 62 7E
7 Hereford, England 52 4N 2 42W
7 Hereford & Worcester, Co., England 52 4N 2 43W
38 Hermosillo, Mexico 29 10N 111 0W
7 Hertfordshire, Co., England 51 51N 0 5W
24 Hida-Sammyaku, Japan 36 30N 137 40E
38 Hidalgo del Parral, Mexico 26 10N 104 50W
7 High Wycombe, Eng. 51 37N 0 45W
8 Highland, Co., Scotland 57 30N 5 0W
36 Hilo, Hawaiian Is. 19 42N 155 4W
22 Himalaya, Mts., Asia 29 0N 84 0E
24 Himeji, Japan 34 50N 134 40E
21 Hindu Kush, Ra., Afghan. 36 0N 71 0E
24 Hiroshima, Japan 37 40N 132 30E
39 Hispaniola, I., W. Indies 19 0N 71 0W
17 Hjørring, Denmark 57 29N 9 59E
27 Hobart, Tasmania 42 50S 147 21E
24 Hokkaido, I., Japan 43 30N 143 0E
39 Holguín, Cuba 20 50N 76 20W
6 Holyhead, Wales 53 18N 4 38W
39 Honduras, Rep. Central America 14 40N 86 30W
17 Hønefoss, Norway 60 10N 10 12E
25 Hong Kong, Br. Crown Colony, Asia 22 11N 14 14E
36 Honolulu, Hawaiian Is. 21 25N 157 55W
24 Honshu, I., Japan 36 0N 138 0E
42 Horn, C., Chile 55 50S 67 30W
17 Horsens, Denmark 55 52N 9 50E
17 Horten, Norway 59 25N 10 32E
13 Hospitalet, Spain 41 21N 2 6E
37 Houston, U.S.A. 29 50N 95 20W
7 Hove, England 50 50N 0 10W
22 Howrah, India 22 37N 88 27E
25 Hsiamen, China 24'30N 118 7E
33 Murambo, Angola 12 42S 15 54W
6 Huddersfield, England 53 38N 1 49W
35 Hudson, B., Canada 60 0N 86 0W
37 Hudson, R., U.S.A. 41 35N 74 0W
35 Hudson Str., Canada 62 0N 70 0W
23 Hue, Vietnam 16 60N 107 35E
13 Huelva, Spain 37 18N 6 57W
13 Huesca, Spain 42 8N 0 25W
27 Hughenden, Australia 20 52S 144 10E
35 Hull, Canada 45 20N 75 40W
6 Hull, England 53 45N 0 20W
6 Humber, R., England 53 42N 0 20W
6 Humberside, Co., Eng. 53 40N 0 30W
11 Hungary, Rep. Europe 47 20N 19 20E
37 Huntingdon, U.S.A. 38 20N 82 30W
35 Huron, L., N. America 45 0N 83 0W
25 Hwang-Ho, R., China 40 50N 107 30E
22 Hyderabad, India 17 10N 78 20E
22 Hyderabad, Pakistan 25 23N 68 36E

I

11 Iaşi, Rumania 47 10N 27 40E
30 Ibadan, Nigeria 7 22N 3 58E
40 Ibaqué, Colombia 4 27N 73 14W
13 Ibiza, I., Spain 39 0N 1 30E
16 Iceland, Rep., Europe 65 0N 19 0W
24 Ichinomiya, Japan 35 20N 136 50E
30 Ife, Nigeria 7 30N 4 31E
23 Iloilo, Philippines, 10 45N 122 33E
25 Inchon, S. Korea 37 30N 126 30E
22 India, St., Asia 23 0N 80 0E
20 Indian Ocean 5 0S 75 0E
37 Indianapolis, U.S.A. 39 42N 86 10W
23 Indonesia, Rep., Asia 5 0S 115 0E
22 Indore, India 22 42N 75 53E
22 Indus, R., Pakistan 28 40N 70 10E
27 Ingham, Australia 18 43S 146 10E
33 Inhambane, Moz. 23 51S 35 29E
8 Inner Hebrides, Is., Scotland 58 0N 7 0W
10 Innsbruck, Austria 47 16N 11 23E
28 Invercargill, N.Z. 46 24S 168 24E
8 Inverness, Scotland 57 29N 4 12W
15 Ionian Sea, Europe 37 30N 17 30E
27 Ipswich, Australia 27 38S 152 37E
7 Ipswich, England 52 4N 1 9E
40 Iquique, Chile 20 19S 70 5W
40 Iquitos, Peru 3 45S 73 10W
15 Iráklion, Greece 35 20N 25 12E
21 Iran, st., Asia 33 0N 53 0E
21 Iraq, st., Asia 33 0N 44 0E
9 Ireland, Rep., Europe 53 0N 8 0W
23 Irian Jaya, Indonesia 4 0S 137 0E
5 Irish Sea, Europe 54 0N 5 0W
19 Irkutsk, U.S.S.R. 52 10N 104 20E
8 Islay, I., Scotland 55 46N 6 10W
31 Ismâ'illa, Egypt 30 47N 32 18E
21 Israel, st., Asia 32 30N 32 30E
21 Istanbul, Turkey 41 0N 29 0E
41 Itabuna, Brazil 14 48S 39 16W
14 Itlay, Rep., Europe 42 0N 13 0E
18 Ivanovo, U.S.S.R. 57 5N 41 0E
30 Ivory Coast, st., W. Africa 7 30N 5 0W

30 Iwo, Nigeria 7 39N 4 9E
18 Izhevsk, U.S.S.R. 56 50N 53 0E
21 Izmir, Turkey 38 25N 27 8E

J

22 Jabalpur, India 23 9N 79 58E
37 Jackson, U.S.A. 32 20N 90 10W
37 Jacksonville, U.S.A. 30 15N 81 38W
13 Jaén, Spain 37 44N 3 43W
22 Jaipur, India 20 51N 86 28E
38 Jalapa, Mexico 19 30N 96 50W
39 Jamaica, I., W. Indies 18 10N 77 30W
35 James, .B, Canada 53 30N 80 30W
22 Jamshedpur, India 22 44N 86 20E
24 Japan, st., Asia 36 0N 136 0E
24 Japan, Sea of, Asia 40 0N 135 0E
41 Jau, Brazil 22 10S 48 30W
23 Java, I., Indonesia 7 0S 110 0E
13 Jerez, Spain 36 41N 6 7W
7 Jersey, I., British Isles 49 13N 2 7W
37 Jersey City, U.S.A. 40 41N 74 8W
21 Jerusalem, Israel 31 47N 35 10E
21 Jidda, Saudi Arabia 21 29N 39 16E
41 João Pessoa, Brazil 7 10S 35 0W
22 Jodhpur, India 26 23N 73 2E
23 Jogjakarta, Indonesia 6 9S 106 49E
33 Johannesburg, S. Africa 26 10S 28 8E
8 John O'Groats, Scot. 58 39N 3 3W
17 Jönköping, Sweden 57 45N 14 10E
21 Jordan, st., Asia 31 0N 36 0E
17 Jotunheimen, Mts., Norway 61 30N 9 0E
41 Juàzeiro do Norte, Brazil 7 10S 39 18W
41 Juiz de Fora, Brazil 21 43S 43 19W
22 Jullundur, India 31 20N 75 40E
34 Juneau, Alaska 58 21N 134 20W
8 Jura, I., Scotland 56 0N 5 50W
12 Jura, Mts., Europe 46 35N 6 5E
40 Juruá, R., Brazil 5 20S 67 40W
16 Jyväskylä, Finland 62 12N 25 47E

K

21 Kabul, Afghanistan 34 28N 69 18E
30 Kaduna, Nigeria 10 30N 7 21E
24 Kagoshima, Japan 31 36N 130 40E
23 Kaifeng, China 34 45N 114 30E
16 Kajaani, Finland 64 17N 27 46E
33 Kalahari, Desert, Africa 24 0S 22 0E
32 Kalemie, Zaïre 5 55S 29 9E
26 Kalgoorlie, Australia 30 40S 121 22E
18 Kalinin, U.S.S.R. 56 55N 35 55E
18 Kaliningrad, U.S.S.R. 54 42N 20 32E
17 Kalmar, Sweden 56 39N 16 22E
18 Kaluga, U.S.S.R. 54 35N 36 10E
32 Kamina, Zaïre 8 45S 25 0E
34 Kamloops, Canada 50 40N 120 20W
32 Kampala, Uganda 0 20N 32 30E
32 Kananga, Zaïre 5 55S 22 18E
24 Kanazawa, Japan 36 30N 136 38E
21 Kandahar, Afghanistan 31 32N 65 30E
18 Kandalaksha, U.S.S.R. 67 9N 32 30E
22 Kandy, Sri Lanka 7 18N 80 43E
30 Kano, Nigeria 12 0N 8 30E
22 Kanpur, India 26 35N 80 20E
37 Kansas City, U.S.A. 39 0N 94 37W
25 Kaohsiung, Taiwan 22 35N 120 16E
22 Karachi, Pakistan 24 53N 67 0E
18 Karaganda, U.S.S.R. 49 50N 73 0E
22 Karakorum, Mts., India 35 20N 78 0E
21 Karbala, Iraq 32 47N 44 3E
33 Kariba, L. Zambia-Rhodesia 16 40S 28 20E
10 Karl-Marx-Stadt, E. Germany 50 50N 12 55E
17 Karlskrona, Sweden 56 12N 15 42E
10 Karlsruhe, W. Germany 49 3N 8 23E
17 Karlstad, Sweden 59 24N 13 35E
32 Kasai, R., Zaïre 8 20S 22 0E
10 Kassel, W. Germany 51 19N 9 32E
26 Katherine, Australia 14 27S 132 20E
22 Katmandu, Nepal 27 45N 85 12E
27 Katoomba, Australia 33 30N 150 0E
11 Katowice Poland, 50 17N 19 5E
30 Katsina, Nigeria 7 10N 9 20E
17 Kattegat, Str., Denmark 56 50N 11 20E
18 Kaunas, U.S.S.R. 54 54N 23 54E
24 Kawaguchi, Japan 35 52N 138 45E
24 Kawasaki, Japan 35 40N 139 45E
28 Kawerau, N.Z. 38 7S 176 42E
18 Kazan, U.S.S.R. 55 48N 49 3E
15 Kazanlŭk, Bulgaria 42 38N 25 35E
33 Keetmanshoop, S.W. Africa 26 35S 18 8E
16 Keflavik, Iceland 64 2N 22 35W
6 Keighley, England 53 52N 1 54W
18 Kemerovo, U.S.S.R. 55 20N 85 50W
16 Kemi, Finland 65 48N 24 43E
34 Kenora, Canada 49 50N 94 35W
7 Kent, Co., England 51 12N 0 40E
32 Kenya, st., E. Africa 0 5N 37 0E
3 Kerguelen, I., Indian Oc. 48 30S 69 40E
15 Kérkira, I., Greece 39 40N 19 50E
28 Kermadec Is., Pacific Oc. 31 8S 175 16W
21 Kerman, Iarn 30 15N 57 1E
21 Kermanshah, Iran 34 23N 47 0E
9 Kerry, Co., Ireland 52 7N 9 35W
37 Key West, U.S.A. 24 40N 82 0W
19 Kharbarovsk, U.S.S.R. 48 20N 135 0E
18 Kharkov, U.S.S.R. 49 58N 36 20E
31 Khartoum = El Kharṭûm
15 Khaskovo, Bulgaria 41 56N 25 30E
18 Kherson, U.S.S.R. 46 35N 32 35E
15 Khíos, I., Greece 38 23N 29 0E
22 Khulna, Bangladesh 22 45N 89 34E
10 Kiel, W. Germany 54 16N 10 8E
15 Kikládhes, Is., Greece 37 50N 25 0E
9 Kildare, Co., Ireland 53 10N 6 50W
32 Kilimanjaro, Mt., Kenya 3 4S 37 21E
9 Kilkenny & Co., Ireland 52 40N 7 17W
9 Killarney, Ireland 52 2N 9 30W
8 Kilmarnock, Scotland 55 36N 4 30W
33 Kimberley, S. Africa 28 43N 24 46E
27 King I., Australia 39 40S 144 0E
6 King's Lynn, England 52 45N 0 25E
35 Kingston, Canada 44 20N 76 30W
32 Kinshasha, Zaïre 4 20N 15 15E
19 Kirensk, U.S.S.R. 57 50N 107 55E
25 Kirin, China 43 50N 126 38E
8 Kirkcaldy, Scotland 56 7N 3 10W
35 Kirkland Lake, Canada 48 15N 80 0W
21 Kirkuk, Iraq 35 30N 44 21E
8 Kirkwall, Scotland 58 59N 2 59W
18 Kirov, U.S.S.R. 58 25N 49 40E
18 Kirovogard, U.S.S.R. 48 35N 32 20E
16 Kiruna, Sweden 67 50N 20 20E
32 Kisangani, Zaïre 0 41N 25 11E
18 Kiselevsk, U.S.S.R. 54 5N 86 6E
18 Kishinev, U.S.S.R. 47 1N 28 50E
29 Kismayu, Somalia 0 20S 42 30E
24 Kitakyúshú, Japan 33 50N 130 50E
35 Kitchener, Canada 43 30N 80 30W
33 Kitwe, Zambia 12 50S 28 0E
18 Kiyev, U.S.S.R. 50 30N 30 28E
10 Klagenfurt, Austria 46 38N 14 20E
37 Knoxville, U.S.A. 35 58N 83 57W
24 Kōbe, Japan 34 45N 135 10E
17 København, (Copenhagen) Denmark 55 41N 12 34E
10 Koblenz, W. Germany 50 21N 7 36E
24 Kōchi, Japan 33 30N 133 35E
16 Kokkola, Finlnad 63 50N 23 8E
17 Kolding, Denmark 55 30N 9 29E
22 Kolhapur, India 16 43N 74 15E
10 Köln, W. Germany 50 56N 9 58E
18 Kolomna, U.S.S.R. 55 8N 38 45E
32 Kolwezi, Zaïre 10 40S 25 25E
19 Komsomolsk, U.S.S.R. 50 30N 137 0E
18 Kopeysk, U.S.S.R. 54 55N 61 31E
15 Korab, Mt., Y-slav. 41 44N 20 40E
24 Kōriyama, Japan 37 10N 140 18E
27 Kosciusko, Mt., Australia 36 27S 148 16E
11 Kosice, Czechoslovakia 48 42N 21 15E
18 Kostroma, U.S.S.R. 57 50N 41 58E
25 Kowloon, Hong Kong 22 25N 114 10E
15 Kragujevac, Yugoslavia 44 2N 20 56E
11 Krakow, Poland 50 4N 19 57E
18 Krasnodar, U.S.S.R. 45 5N 38 50E
18 Krasnovodsk, U.S.S.R. 50 0N 52 52E
19 Krasnoyarsk, U.S.S.R. 56 8N 93 0E
18 Kremenchug, U.S.S.R. 49 5N 33 25E
17 Kristiansand, Norway 58 9N 8 1E
17 Kristiansund, Norway 63 10N 7 45E
16 Kristinestad, Finland 62 16N 21 21E
15 Kriti, I., (Crete) Greece 35 15N 25 0E
18 Krivoy Rog, U.S.S.R. 47 51N 33 20E
33 Krugersdorp, S. Africa 26 5S 27 46E
23 Krung Thep (Bangkok) Thailand 13 45N 100 31E
23 Kuala Lumpur, Malasyia 3 9N 101 41E
24 Kumamoto, Japan 32 45N 130 45E
30 Kumasi, Ghana 6 41N 1 38W
32 Kumba, Cameroon 4 36N 9 24E
25 Kunlun Shan, Asia 36 0N 86 30E
25 Kunming, China 25 0N 102 45E
26 Kununurra, Australia 15 40S 128 39E
16 Kuopio, Finland 62 53N 27 35E
24 Kurashiki, Japan 34 40N 133 50E
24 Kure, Japan 33 15N 133 15E
18 Kurgan, U.S.S.R. 55 30N 65 0E
18 Kursk, U.S.S.R. 51 42N 36 11E
18 Kustanai, U.S.S.R. 53 20N 63 45E
21 Kuwait = Al Kuwayt
21 Kuwait, st., Asia 29 30N 47 30E
18 Kuybyshev, U.S.S.R. 53 20N 57 0E
25 Kwangchow, China 23 10N 113 10E
25 Kweiyang, China 26 30N 106 35E
8 Kyle of Lochalsh, Scotland 57 17N 5 43 W
24 Kyushu, I., Japan 32 30N 131 0E

L

39 La Ceiba, Honduras 15 40N 86 50W
13 La Coruña, Spain 43 20N 8 25W
39 La Habana, Cuba 23 8N 82 22W
13 La Linea de la Concepción, Spain 36 15N 5 23W
40 La Paz, Bolivia 16 20S 68 10W
38 La Paz, Mexico 24 10N 110 20W
38 La Piedad, Mexico 20 20N 102 1W
42 La Plata, Argentina 35 0S 57 55W
12 La Rochelle, France 46 10N 1 9W
39 La Romana, Dominican Rep. 18 27N 68 57W
42 La Serena, Chile 29 55S 71 10W
14 La Spézia, Italy 44 8N 9 48E
35 Labrador, Reg., Canada 53 20N 61 0W
23 Labuan, I. Malaysia 5 15N 115 38W
22 Laccadive Is., Indian Oc. 10 0N 72 30E
9 Lagan, R., N. Ireland 54 35N 5 55W
30 Lagos, Nigeria 6 25N 3 27E
13 Lagos, Portugal 37 5N 8 41W
22 Lahore, Pakistan 31 32N 74 22E
17 Lahti, Finland 60 59N 25 45E
37 Lakewood, U.S.A. 41 28N 81 50W
6 Lancashire, Co., England 53 5N 2 30W
6 Lancaster, England 54 3N 2 48W
25 Lanchow, China 36 0N 103 50E
7 Land's End, England 50 4N 5 43W
12 Langrse, France 47 52N 5 20E
37 Lansing, U.S.A. 42 47N 84 32W
9 Laois, Co., Ireland 53 0N 7 20W
23 Laos, st., Asia 17 45N 105 0E
19 Lapter Sea, 'S.S.R. 76 0N 125 0E
14 L'Aquila, Italy 42 21N 13 24E
36 Laredo, U.S.A. 27 34N 99 29W
15 Lárisa, Greece 39 38N 22 28E
17 Larvik, Norway 59 4N 10 0E
30 Las Palmas, Canary Is. 28 10N 15 28W
36 Las Vegas, U.S.A. 36 10N 115 5W
27 Launceston, Australia 41 24S 147 8E
10 Lausanne, Switzerland 46 32N 6 38E
12 Le Havre, France 49 30N 0 5E
12 Le Mans, France 48 0N 0 12E
7 Leamington, England 52 18N 1 32W
21 Lebanon, st., Asia 34 0N 36 0E
15 Lecce, Italy 40 20N 18 10E
6 Leeds, England 53 48N 1 34W
39 Leeward Is., W. Indies 16 30N 63 30W
14 Leghorn = Livorno
7 Leicester & Co., England 52 39N 1 9W
10 Leipzig, E. Germany 51 20N 12 23E
8 Leith, Scotland 55 55N 3 11W
9 Leitrim, Co., Ireland 54 8N 8 0W
10 Léman, L. Switzerland 46 26N 6 30E
18 Leningrad, U.S.S.R. 59 55N 30 20E
18 Leninsk Kuznetskiy U.S.S.R. 55 10N 86 10E
38 León, Mexico 21 7N 101 30W
39 León, Nicaragua 12 20N 86 51W
13 León, Spain 42 38N 5 34W
13 Lérida, Spain 41 37N 0 39E
8 Lerwick, Scotland 60 10N 1 10W
33 Lesotho, st., Africa 29 40S 28 0E
15 Lésvos, I., Greece 26 0N 39 15E
34 Lethbridge, Canada 49 45N 112 45W
28 Levin, N.Z. 40 37S 175 18E
21 Levkósia, Cyprus 35 10N 33 25E
8 Lewis, I., Scotland 58 10N 6 40W
37 Lexington, U.S.A. 38 6N 84 30W
25 Lhasa, Tibet, China 29 40N 91 10E
30 Liberia, st., W. Africa 6 30N 9 30W
32 Libreville, Gabon 0 25N 9 26E
31 Libya, st., N. Africa 28 30N 17 30E
10 Liechtenstein, st., Europe 47 8N 9 35E
9 Liffey, R., Ireland 53 21N 6 20W
9 Lifford, Ireland 54 50N 7 30W
14 Ligurian Sea, Europe 43 20N 9 0E
32 Likasi, Zaïre 10 55S 26 48E
12 Lille, France 50 38N 3 3E
17 Lillehammer, Norway 61 8N 10 30E
33 Lilongwe, Malawi 14 0S 33 48E
40 Lima, Peru 12 0S 77 0W
37 Lima, U.S.A. 40 42N 84 5W
9 Limerick & Co., Ireland 52 40N 8 38W
15 Límnos, I., Greece 39 50N 25 15E
12 Limoges, France 45 50N 1 15E
39 Limón, Costa Rica 10 0N 83 2W
33 Limpopo, R. Africa 24 15S 32 45E
13 Linares, Spain 38 10N 3 40W
6 Lincoln & Co., England 53 11N 0 20W
37 Lincoln, U.S.A. 40 50N 96 42W
17 Linköping, Sweden 58 28N 15 36E
8 Linnhe, L., Scotland 56 36N 5 25W
10 Linz, Austria 48 18N 14 18E
14 Lípari, Is., Italy 38 40N 15 0E
18 Lipetsk, U.S.S.R. 52 45N 39 35E
13 Lisboa, Portugal 38 42N 9 10W
9 Lisburn, N. Ireland 54 30N 6 2W
27 Lismore, Australia 28 44S 153 21E
9 Listowel, Ierland 52 27N 9 30W
37 Little Rock ,U.S.A. 34 41N 92 10W
6 Liverpool, England 53 25N 3 0W
33 Livingstone, Zambia 17 50N 25 50E
14 Livorno, Italy 43 32N 10 18E
7 Lizard, Pt., England 49 57N 5 11W
14 Ljubljana, Yugoslavia 46 4N 14 33E
33 Lobito, Angola 12 18S 13 35E
40 Llanos, S. America 3 25N 71 35W
11 Lódz, Poland 51 45N 19 27E
16 Lofoten, Is., Norway 68 20N 14 0E
13 Logroño, Spain 42 28N 2 32W
12 Loire, R., France 47 25N 0 20W
23 Lombok, I., Indonesia 8 35S 116 20E
30 Lomé, Togo 6 9N 1 20E
35 London, Canada 43 0N 81 15W
7 London, England 51 30N 0 5W
9 Londonderry, N. Ireland 55 0N 7 20W
42 Londrina, Brazil 23 0S 51 10W
36 Long Beach, U.S.A. 33 46N 118 12W
37 Long I., U.S.A. 40 50N 73 20W
9 Longford, & Co., Ire. 53 43N 7 50W
13 Lorca, Spain 37 41N 1 42W
12 Lorient, France 47 45N 3 23W
36 Los Angeles, U.S.A. 34 0N 118 10W
8 Lothian, Co., Scotland 55 55N 3 15W
37 Louisville, U.S.A. 38 15N 85 45W
33 Lourenço Marques = Maputo, Mozambique 25 57S 32 34E
9 Louth, Co., Ireland 53 55N 6 30W
28 Lower Hutt, N.Z. 41 10S 174 55E
7 Lowestoft, England 52 29N 1 44E
25 Loyang, China 34 40N 112 28E
32 Lualaba, R., Zaïre 5 45S 26 50E
32 Luanda, Angola 8 58S 13 9E
33 Luanshya, Zambia 13 20S 28 8E
36 Lubbock, U.S.A. 33 40N 102 0W
11 Lublin, Poland 51 12N 22 38E
33 Lubumbashi, Zaïre 11 32S 27 28E
14 Lucca, Italy 43 50N 10 30E
25 Luchow, China 28 54N 105 17E
22 Lucknow, India 26 50N 81 0E
33 Lüderitz, S.W. Africa 26 37S 15 9E
22 Ludhiana, India 30 57N 75 56E
13 Lugo, Spain 43 2N 7 35W
16 Luleå, Sweden 65 35N 22 10E
33 Lusaka, Zambia 15 25S 28 15E
25 Lu-Ta, China 39 0N 121 31E
7 Luton, England 51 53N 0 24W
10 Luxembourg, st. Europe 50 0N 6 0E
10 Luzern, Switzerland 47 3N 8 18E
23 Luzon, I. Philippines 16 30N 121 30E
18 Lvov, U.S.S.R. 49 40N 24 0E
22 Lyallpur, Pakistan 31 30N 73 5E
16 Lycksele, Sweden 64 38N 18 40E
37 Lynchburg, U..SA. 37 23N 79 10W
12 Lyon, France 45 46N 4 50E
28 Lyttleton, N.Z. 43 35S 172 44E

M

25 Macau, China 22 16N 113 35E
41 Maceió, Brazil 9 40S 35 41W
9 Macgillycuddy's Reeks, Mts., Ireland 52 2N 9 45W
27 Mackay, Australia 21 36S 148 39E
34 Mackenzie, R., Can. 69 10N 134 20W
37 Macon, U.S.A. 32 50N 83 37W
9 Macroom, Ireland 51 54N 8 57W
33 Madagascar, st., Africa 19 0S 46 0E
30 Madeira, Is. Atlantic Oc. 32 50N 17 0W
40 Madeira, R., Brazil 5 30S 61 20W
37 Madison, U.S.A. 43 5N 89 25W
22 Madras, India 13 8N 80 19E
13 Madrid, Spain 40 25N 3 45W
22 Madurai, India 9 55N 78 10E
24 Maebashi, Japan 36 30N 139 0E
40 Magdalena, R., Colombia 8 30N 74 0W
10 Magdeburg, E. Germany 52 8N 11 36E
18 Magnitogorsk, U.S.S.R. 53 20N 59 0E
7 Maidstone, England 51 16N 0 31E
31 Maiduguri, Nigeria 12 0N 13 20E
10 Mainz, W. Germany 50 0N 8 17E
27 Maitland, Australia 32 44S 151 36E
23 Makasar, Str. of, Indon. 1 0S 118 20E
18 Makeyevka, U.S.S.R. 48 0N 38 0E
21 Makkah (Mecca), Saudi Arabia 21 30N 39 54E
23 Malacca, Str. of, Indonesia 3 0N 101 0E
13 Malaga, Spain 36 43N 4 23W
33 Malagasy Rep. st. = Madagascar 19 0S 46 0E
33 Malawi, L., Malawi 12 0S 34 30E
33 Malawi, st., Africa 13 0S 34 0E
23 Malaysia, Fed. of, Asia 5 23N 110 0E
22 Maldive Is., Indian Oc. 6 50N 73 0E
30 Mali, st., W. Africa 17 0N 4 0W
9 Malin Hd., Ireland 55 18N 7 16W
8 Mallaig, Scotland 57 0N 5 50W
13 Mallorca, I., Spain 39 30N 3 0E
9 Mallow, Ireland 52 8N 8 40W
17 Malmö, Sweden 55 33N 13 8E
14 Malta, st. Mediterranean Sea 35 50N 14 30E
6 Man, I. of, U.K. 54 15N 4 30W
23 Manado, Indonesia 1 40N 125 45E
39 Managua, Nicaragua 12 0N 86 20W
40 Manaus, Brazil 3 0S 60 0W
6 Manchester, England 53 30N 2 15W
37 Manchester, U.S.A. 42 58N 71 29W
22 Mandale, Burma 22 0N 96 10E
23 Manila, Philippines 14 40N 121 3E
34 Manitoba, L., Canada 50 40N 98 30W
40 Manizales, Colombia 5 10N 75 30W
10 Mannheim, W. Ger. 49 28N 8 29E
6 Mansfield, England 53 8N 1 12W
14 Mantova, (Mantua) Italy 45 10N 10 47E
28 Manukau, N.Z. 37 0S 174 50E
39 Manzanillo, Cuba 20 20N 77 10W
33 Maputo, Mozambique 25 57S 32 34E
42 Mar del Plata, Argentina 38 0S 57 30W
40 Maracaibo, Venezuela 10 37N 71 45W
40 Maracaibo, L. de, Ven. 9 40N 71 30W
40 Maracay, Venezuela 10 20N 67 35W
40 Margarita, I. de, Ven. 11 0N 64 0W
7 Margate, England 51 23N 1 24E
28 Maria van Diemen, C., N.Z. 34 29S 172 40E
3 Mariana Is., Pacific Oc. 17 0N 145 0E
39 Marianao, Cuba 23 8N 82 24W
14 Maribor, Yugoslavia 46 36N 15 40E
41 Marilia, Brazil 22 0S 50 0W
42 Maringá, Brazil 23 35S 51 50W
2 Marquesas Is., Pacific Oc. 9 30S 140 0W
30 Marrakech, Morocco 31 40N 8 0W
12 Marseille, France 43 18N 5 23E
3 Marshall Is., Pacific Oc. 9 0N 171 0E
39 Martinique, I., Fr. W. Indies 14 40N 61 0W
27 Maryborough, Austral. 25 31S 152 37E
39 Masaya, Nicaragua 12 0N 86 7W
21 Masqat, Oman 23 37N 58 36E
12 Massif Central, Mts., Fr. 45 30N 2 21E
28 Masterton, N.Z. 40 56S 175 39E
32 Matadi, Zaïre 5 52S 13 31E
39 Matagalpa, Nicaragua 13 10N 85 40W
38 Matamoros, Mexico 25 50N 97 30W
39 Matanzas, Cuba 23 0N 81 40W
24 Matsue, Japan 35 25N 133 10E
24 Matsuyama, Japan 33 45N 132 45E
30 Mauritania, st., Africa 20 0N 10 0W
29 Mauritius, st., Indian Oc. 20 0S 57 0E
39 Mayagüez, Puerto Rico 18 11N 67 8W
18 Maykop, U.S.S.R. 44 35N 40 25E
9 Mayo, Co., Ireland 53 47N 9 7W
38 Mazatlán, Mexico 23 10N 106 30W
32 Mbandaka, Zaïre 0 1S 18 18E
9 Meath, Co., Ireland 53 32N 6 40W
21 Mecca = Makkah
23 Medan, Indonesia 3 40N 98 38E
40 Medellín, Colombia 6 20N 75 45W
34 Medicine Hat, Canada 50 0N 110 45W
21 Medina = Al Madinah
4 Mediterranean Sea, Europe 35 0N 15 0E
22 Meerut, India 29 1N 77 50E
30 Meknès, Morocco 33 57N 5 39W
23 Mekong, R., Asia 18 0N 104 15E
27 Melbourne, Australia 37 40S 145 0E
30 Melilla Sp. Morocco 35 21N 2 57W
18 Melitopol, U.S.S.R. 46 50N 35 22E
26 Melville I., Australia 11 30S 131 0E
37 Memphis, U.S.A. 35 7N 90 0W
6 Menai, Str., Wales 53 7N 4 20W
42 Mendoza, Argentina 32 50S 68 52W
13 Menorca, I., Spain 40 0N 4 0E
42 Mercedes, Uruguay 33 12S 58 0W
23 Mergui Arch, Burma 11 30N 97 30E
38 Mérida, Mexico 20 50N 89 40W
6 Merseyside, Co., England 53 30N 3 0W
7 Merthyr Tydfil, Wales 51 45N 3 23W
14 Messina, & Str., Italy 38 10N 15 32E
33 Messina, S. Africa 22 20S 30 12E
12 Metz, France 49 8N 6 10E
38 Mexicali, Mexico 32 40N 115 30W
38 Mexico, st., America 20 0N 100 0N
38 Mexico, G. of, Central America 25 0N 90 0W
38 Mexico City, Mexico 19 20N 99 10W
37 Miami, U.S.A. 25 52N 80 15W
18 Miass, U.S.S.R. 54 59N 60 6E
37 Michigan, L., N. America 44 0N 87 0W
7 Mid Glamorgan, Co., Wales 51 35N 3 30W
33 Middelburg, S. Africa 31 30S 25 0E
6 Middlesbrough, England 54 34N 1 13W
36 Midland, U.S.A. 32 0N 102 3W
2 Midway I., Pacific Oc. 28 0N 178 0W
13 Mieres, Spain 43 18N 5 48W
14 Milano, (Milan) Italy 45 28N 9 10E
27 Mildura, Australia 34 8S 142 7E
7 Milford Haven, Wales 51 43N 5 2W
37 Milwaukee, U.S.A. 43 9N 87 58W
38 Minatitlán, Mexico 17 58N 94 35W
23 Mindanao, I., Philippines 8 0N 125 0E
37 Minneapolis, U.S.A. 44 58N 93 20W
18 Minsk, U.S.S.R. 53 52N 27 30E
11 Miskolc, Hungary 48 7N 20 50E
37 Mississippi, R., U.S.A. 41 0N 91 0W
36 Missouri, R., U.S.A. 38 40N 91 45W
9 Mizen Hd., Ireland 51 27N 9 50W
37 Mobile, U.S.A. 30 41N 88 3W
32 Mobutu Sese Seko, L., Africa 1 30N 31 0E
33 Moçambique, Mozam. 15 3S 40 42E
33 Moçambique, st. Africa 14 45S 38 30E
33 Moçâmedes, Angola 16 35S 12 30E
14 Módena, Italy 44 39N 10 55E
27 Moe, Australia 38 12S 146 19E
29 Mogadishu, Somalia 2 2N 45 25E
18 Mogilev, U.S.S.R. 53 55N 30 18E
17 Mölndal, Sweden 57 40N 12 3E
32 Mombasa, Kenya 4 0S 39 35E
12 Monaco, principality, Europe 43 36N 7 23E
9 Monaghan & Co., 54 15N 6 58W
38 Monclova, Mexico 26 50N 101 30W
35 Moncton, Canada 46 7N 64 51W
25 Mongolia, Rep., Asia 47 0N 103 0E
30 Monrovia, Liberia 6 18N 10 47W
12 Monte Carlo, Monaco 43 46N 7 23E
39 Montego Bay, Jamaica 18 30N 78 0W
38 Monterrey, Mexico 25 40N 100 30W
41 Montes Claros, Brazil 16 30S 43 50W
42 Montevideo, Uruguay 34 50S 56 11W
37 Montgomery, U.S.A. 32 20N 86 20W
12 Montluçon, France 46 22N 2 36E
12 Montpellier, France 43 37N 3 52E
35 Montreal, Canada 45 31N 73 34W
12 Montreuil, France 50 27N 1 45W
8 Montrose, Scotland 56 43N 2 28W
34 Moose Jaw, Canada 50 30N 105 30W
15 Morava, R., Cz. 49 50N 16 50E
8 Moray Firth, Scotland 57 50N 3 30W
6 Morecambe, England 54 5N 2 52W
38 Morelia, Mexico 19 40N 101 11W
30 Morocco, st., N. Africa 32 0N 5 0W
18 Moscow = Moskva
10 Mosel, R., Germany 49 48N 6 45E
16 Mosjøen, Norway 65 52N 13 20E
18 Moskva, U.S.S.R. 55 45N 37 35E
17 Moss, Norway 59 27N 10 40E
33 Mosselbaai, S. Africa 34 11S 22 8E
21 Mosul = Al Mawsil
17 Motala, Sweden 58 32N 15 1E
8 Motherwell, Scotland 55 48N 4 0W
27 Mount Gambier, Australia 37 38S 140 44E
27 Mount Isa, Australia 20 42S 139 26E
26 Mount Magnet, Australia 28 2S 117 47E
9 Mourne, Mts., N. Ire. 54 10N 6 0W
33 Mozambique Chan., Africa 20 0S 39 0E
33 Mozambique, Rep. Africa 23 30S 32 30E
32 Mtwara, Tanzania 10 20S 40 20E
33 Mufulira, Zambia 12 30S 28 0E
12 Mulhouse, France 47 44N 7 20E
8 Mull, I., Scotland 56 27N 6 0W
9 Mullinger, Ireland 53 31N 7 20W
22 Multan, Pakistan 30 15N 71 30E
10 Munchen, W. Germany 48 8N 11 33E
10 Münster, W. Germany 51 58N 7 37E
13 Murcia, Spain 38 2N 1 10W
18 Murmansk, U.S.S.R. 68 57N 33 10E
24 Muroran, Japan 42 25N 141 0E
27 Murray, R., Australia 35 50S 147 40E
21 Muscat = Masqat
32 Mweru, L., Zambia 9 0S 29 0E
22 Mysore, India 13 15N 77 0E

N

9 Naas, Ireland 53 12N 6 40W
24 Nagano, Japan 36 40N 138 10E
24 Nagasaki, Japan 32 47N 129 50E
24 Nagoya, Japan 35 10N 136 50E
22 Nagpur, India 21 8N 79 10E
32 Nairobi, Kenya 1 20S 36 50E
32 Nakuru, Kenya 0 15S 36 5E
16 Namsos, Norway 64 28N 11 35E
25 Nan Shan, China 38 0N 98 0E
34 Nanaimo, Canada 49 10N 124 0W
12 Nancy, France 48 42N 6 12E
25 Nanking, China 32 10N 118 50E
12 Nantes, France 47 12N 1 33W
28 Napier, N.Z. 39 30S 176 56E
14 Napoli (Naples) Italy 40 40N 14 5E
12 Narbonne, France 43 11N 3 0E
22 Narmada, R., India 22 40N 77 30E
27 Narrandera, Australia 34 42S 146 31E
26 Narrogin, Australia 32 58S 117 14E
16 Narvik, Norway 68 28N 17 35E
37 Nashville, U.S.A. 36 12N 86 46W
22 Nasik, India 20 2N 73 50E
39 Nassau, Bahamas 25 0N 77 30W
31 Nasser, L., Egypt 23 0N 32 30E
17 Nässjö, Sweden 57 38N 14 45E
41 Natal, Brazil 5 47S 35 13W
38 Navojoa, Mexico 27 0N 109 30W
15 Naxos, I., Greece 37 5N 25 30E
31 Ndjamena, Chad 12 4N 15 8E
33 Ndola, Zambia 13 0S 28 34E
9 Neagh, L., N. Ireland 54 35N 6 25W
42 Negro, R., Brazil 0 25S 64 0W
28 Nelson, N.Z. 41 18S 173 16E
9 Nenagh, Ireland 52 52N 8 11W
22 Nepal, St., Asia 28 0N 84 30E
8 Ness, L., Scotland 57 15N 4 30W
10 Netherlands, King. Europe 52 0N 5 30E
12 Nevers, France 47 0N 3 9E
37 New Bedford, U.S.A. 41 40N 70 52W
28 New Brighton, N.Z. 43 29S 172 43E
3 New Britain, I., Pacific Oc. 6 0S 151 0E
3 New Caledonia, I., Pacific Oc. 21 0S 165 0E
27 New England Ra., Australia 29 30S 152 0E
3 New Guinea, I., Australasia 4 0S 136 0E
37 New Haven, U.S.A. 41 20N 72 54W
3 New Hebrides Is., Pacific Oc. 15 0S 168 0E
3 New Ireland, I., Pacific Oc. 3 0S 151 30E
27 New Norfolk, Australia 44 46S 147 2E
37 New Orleans, U.S.A. 30 0N 90 0W

28 New Plymouth, N.Z. 39 4S 174 5E
39 New Providence, I., Bahamas 25 0N 77 30W
37 New York, U.S.A. 40 45N 74 0W
34 New Zealand, st., 40 0S 175 0E
37 Newark, U.S.A. 40 41N 74 12W
27 Newcastle, Australia 32 52S 151 49E
6 Newcastle, England 54 58N 1 37W
6 Newcastle-under-Lyme, England 53 2N 2 15W
35 Newfoundland, I., Can. 48 28N 56 0W
37 Newhaven, England, 50 47N 0 4E
37 Newmarket, England 52 15N 0 23E
4 Newport, Wales 52 1N 4 51W
37 Newport Mews, U.S.A. 37 0N 76 25W
37 Newtownards, N. Ire. 54 37N 5 40W
37 Niagara Falls, N. Amer. 43 5N 79 5W
37 Niamey, Niger 13 27N 2 6E
39 Nicaragua, st. Central America 11 40N 85 30W
12 Nice, France 43 42N 7 14E
21 Nicobar, Is., India 9 0N 93 0E
21 Nicosia = Levkôsia
30 Niger, st., Africa 13 30N 10 0E
30 Niger, R., Africa 13 35N 7 0E
30 Nigeria, st., W. Africa 8 30N 8 0E
24 Niigata, Japan 37 58N 139 0E
18 Nijmegen, Netherlands 51 50N 5 52E
18 Nikolayev, U.S.S.R. 46 58N 32 7E
31 Nile, R., Egypt 27 30N 30 30E
12 Nîmes, France 43 50N 4 23E
25 Ningpo, China 29 50N 121 30E
25 Nipigon, L., Canada 49 40N 88 30W
15 Niš, Yugoslavia 43 19N 21 58E
24 Nishinomiya, Japan 34 45N 135 20E
41 Niteroi, Brazil 22 52S 43 0W
18 Nizhniy Tagil, U.S.S.R. 57 45N 60 0E
38 Nogales, Meixco 31 36N 94 29W
4 Nome, Alaska 64 35N 165 40W
6 Norfolk, Co., England 52 39N 1 0E
37 Norfolk, U.S.A. 36 40N 76 0W
3 Norfolk I., Pacific Oc. 28 58S 168 3E
26 Normanton, Australia 17 40S 141 10E
17 Norrköping, Sweden 58 35N 16 10E
34 North Battleford, Canada 52 50N 108 10W
35 North Bay, Canada 46 20N 79 30W
5 North Chan., British Isles 55 0N 5 30W
28 North I., N.Z. 38 0S 175 0E
25 North Korea, St., Asia 40 0N 127 0E
4 North Sea, Europe 55 0N 4 9E
8 North Uist, I., Scotland 57 40N 7 15W
6 North York Moors, England 54 25N 0 50W
6 North Yorkshire, Co., England 54 20N 1 30W
26 Northam, Australia 31 55S 116 42W
6 Northampton & Co., 52 14N 0 54W
9 Northern Ireland, United Kingdom 54 45N 7 0W
6 Northumberland, Co., England 55 12N 2 0W
16 Norway, King. Europe 67 0N 11 0E
6 Norwich, England 52 38N 1 17E
6 Nottingham & Co., 52 57N 1 10W
3 Nouméa, New Caledonia 22 17S 166 30E
33 Nova Lisboa, see Huambo, Angola 12 42S 15 54W
14 Novara, Italy 45 27N 8 36E
18 Novaya Zemlya, Is. U.S.S.R. 75 0N 56 0E
18 Novgorod, U.S.S.R. 58 30N 31 25E
15 Novi Sad, Yugoslavia 45 18N 19 52E
18 Novokuznetsk, U.S.S.R. 55 0N 83 5E
18 Novomoskovsk, U.S.S.R. 54 5N 38 15E
18 Novorossiysk, U.S.S.R. 44 43N 37 52E
18 Novosibirsk, U.S.S.R. 55 0N 83 5E
38 Nueva Rosita, Mexico 28 0N 101 20W
6 Nuneaton, England 53 32 1 29W
10 Nürnberg, W. Germany 49 26N 11 5E
33 Nyasa, L., Africa 12 0S 34 30E

O
36 Oahu, I., Hawaiian Is. 21 30N 158 0W
37 Oak Ridge, U.S.A. 36 1N 84 5W
36 Oakland, U.S.A. 37 50N 122 18W
28 Oamaru, N.Z. 45 5S 170 59E
38 Oaxaca, Mexico 17 2N 96 40W
18 Ob, R., U.S.S.R. 62 40N 66 0E
8 Oban, Scotland 56 25N 5 30W
40 Occidental, Cordillera, Colombia 5 0N 76 0W
16 Odense, Denmark 55 26N 10 26E
18 Odessa, U.S.S.R. 41 30S 30 45E
10 Odra, R. Poland 52 40N 14 28E
9 Offaly, Co., Ireland 53 15N 7 30W
30 Ogbomosho, Nigeria 8 1N 3 29E
36 Ogden, U.S.A. 41 13N 112 1W
37 Ohio, st. 39 40N 80 50W
24 Ôita, Japan 33 15N 131 36E
33 Okavango Swamps, Botswana 19 30S 23 0E
24 Okayama, Japan 34 40N 133 44E
24 Okazaki, Japan 34 36N 137 0E
19 Okhotsk, Sea of, Asia 55 0N 145 0E
37 Oklahoma City, U.S.A. 35 25N 97 30W
17 Öland, I., Sweden 56 45N 16 50E
10 Oldenburg, W. Germany 53 10N 8 10E
6 Oldham, England 53 33N 2 8W
15 Ólimbos, Oros, (Olympus) Greece 40 6N 22 23E
15 Olympia, Greece 37 39N 21 39E
21 Oman, G. of, S.W. Asia 24 30N 58 30E
21 Oman, Sultanate, Asia 23 0N 58 0E
9 Omagh, N. Ireland 54 36N 7 20W
37 Omaha, U.S.A. 41 15N 96 0W
31 Omdurmân, Sudan 15 40N 32 28E
24 Omiya, Japan 36 0N 139 32E
18 Omsk, U.S.S.R. 55 0N 73 38E
28 Onehunga, N.Z. 36 55N 174 50E
30 Onitsha, Nigeria 6 6N 6 42E
35 Ontario, L., N. America 43 40N 78 0W
11 Oradea, Rumania 47 2N 21 58E
30 Oran, Algeria 36 45N 0 39W

33 Orange, R., S. Africa 29 50S 24 45E
33 Orange, R., S. Africa 28 30S 18 0E
18 Ordzhonikidze, U.S.S.R. 43 0N 44 30E
17 Orebro, Sweden 59 20N 15 18E
18 Orel, U.S.S.R. 52 57N 36 3E
18 Orenburg, U.S.S.R. 52 0N 55 5E
12 Orense, Spain 42 19N 7 55W
12 Orléans, France 47 54N 1 52E
40 Orinoco, R., Venezuela 9 0N 65 30W
40 Orizaba, Mexico 18 50N 97 10W
8 Orkney, Is., Scotland 59 0N 3 0W
37 Orlando, U.S.A. 28 30N 81 25W
16 Örnsköldsvik, Sweden 63 17N 18 50E
18 Orsha, U.S.S.R. 54 30N 30 25E
18 Orsk, U.S.S.R. 51 20N 58 34E
40 Oruro, Bolivia 18 0S 67 19W
24 Osaka, Japan 34 40N 135 30E
30 Oshogbo, Nigeria 7 48N 4 37E
15 Osijek, Yugoslavia 43 34N 18 41E
17 Oskarshamn, Sweden 57 15N 16 25E
17 Oslo, Norway 59 53N 10 52E
16 Östersund, Sweden 63 10N 14 45E
11 Ostrava, Czechoslovakia 49 51N 18 18E
15 Otranto, Str. of, Adriatic Sea 40 15N 18 40E
35 Ottawa, Canada 45 27N 75 42W
30 Ouagadougou, Upper Volta 12 25N 1 30W
30 Oubangi, R., Zaïre 1 0N 17 50E
30 Oujda, Morocco 34 45N 2 0W
16 Oulu, Finland 64 25N 27 30E
4 Ouse, R., England 52 12N 0 7E
8 Outer Hebrides, Is., Scotland
12 Oviedo, Spain 43 25N 5 50W
7 Oxford & Co., 51 45N 1 15W
30 Oyo, Nigeria 7 46N 3 56E

P
38 Pachuca, Mexico 20 10N 98 40W
2 Pacific Ocean 10 0N 140 0W
23 Padang, Indonesia 1 0S 100 20E
14 Pádova, Italy 45 24N 11 52E
8 Paisley, Scotland 55 51N 4 27W
22 Pakistan, St., Asia 30 0N 70 0E
23 Palawan, I., Philippines 10 0N 119 0E
23 Palembang, Indonesia 3 0S 104 50E
12 Palencia, Spain 42 1N 4 34W
14 Palermo, Italy 38 8N 13 20E
13 Palma, Spain 39 33N 2 39E
28 Palmerston North, N.Z. 40 21S 175 39E
40 Palmira, Colombia 3 32N 76 16W
13 Pamplona, Spain 42 48N 1 38W
38 Panama, Panama 9 0N 79 25W
38 Panama, Rep., Central America 9 0N 79 35W
42 Paraguay, R., Paraguay 24 30S 58 20W
42 Paraguay, Rep., S. Amer. 23 0S 57 0W
41 Paramaribo, Surinam 5 50N 55 10W
42 Paraná, Argentina 32 0S 60 30W
42 Paraná, R., Argentine 33 43S 59 15W
12 Paris, France 48 50N 2 20E
27 Parkes, Australia 33 9S 148 11E
14 Parma, Italy 44 50N 10 20E
35 Parry Sound, Canada 45 20N 80 0W
36 Pasadena, U.S.A. 34 5N 118 0W
22 Patna, India 23 35N 85 18E
15 Patrai, Greece 38 14N 21 47E
12 Pau, France 43 19N 0 25W
14 Pavia, Italy 45 10N 9 10E
18 Pavlodar, U.S.S.R. 52 33N 77 0E
15 Pazardzhik, Bulgaria 42 12N 24 20E
11 Pécs, Hungary 46 5N 18 15E
25 Peiping, China 39 50N 116 20E
23 Pekalongan, Indonesia 6 53S 109 40E
42 Pelotas, Brazil 31 42S 52 23W
35 Pembroke, Wales 51 40N 5 0W
23 Penang, I., Malaysia 5 25N 100 15E
25 Pengpu, China 33 0N 117 25E
25 Penki, China 41 20N 123 50E
6 Pennines, Rd., England 54 50N 2 20W
34 Penticton, Canada 49 30N 119 30W
8 Pentland Firth, 58 43N 3 10W
18 Penza, U.S.S.R. 53 15N 45 5E
7 Penzance, England 50 7N 5 32W
37 Peoria, U.S.A. 40 40N 89 40W
40 Pereira, Colombia 4 50N 75 40W
18 Perm, U.S.S.R. 58 0N 56 10E
12 Perpignan, France 42 42N 2 53E
21 Persian G., Asia 27 0N 50 0E
26 Perth, Australia 31 57S 115 52E
8 Perth, Scotland 56 24N 3 27W
40 Peru, Rep., S. America 8 0S 75 0W
14 Perúgia, Italy 43 6N 12 24E
18 Pervouralsk, U.S.S.R. 56 55N 60 0E
14 Pésaro, Italy 43 55N 12 50E
14 Pescara, Italy 42 28N 14 13E
22 Peshawar, Pakistan 34 2N 71 37E
35 Peterboro' Canada 44 20N 78 20W
27 Peterborough, Australia 33 0S 138 45E
7 Peterborough, England 52 35N 0 14W
8 Peterhead, Scotland 57 30N 1 49W
28 Petone, N.Z. 41 13S 174 53E
18 Petropavlovsk, U.S.S.R. 55 0N 69 0E
19 Petropavlovsk-Kamchatskiy, U.S.S.R. 53 16N 159 0E
18 Petrozavodsk, U.S.S.R. 61 41N 34 20E
23 Phan Bho Ho Chi Minh, Vietnam 10 58N 106 40E
37 Philadelphia, U.S.A. 40 0N 75 10W
23 Philippines, Rep., Asia 12 0N 123 0E
23 Phnom Penh, Cambodia 11 33N 104 55E
36 Phoenix, U.S.A. 33 40N 112 10W
2 Phoenix Is., Pacific Oc. 3 30S 172 0W
14 Piacenza, Italy 45 3N 9 41E
28 Picton, N.Z. 41 18S 174 3E
38 Piedras Negras, Mexico 28 35N 100 35W
33 Pietermaritzburg, S. Africa 23 54S 29 25E
33 Pietersburg, S. Africa 23 54S 29 25E

39 Pinar del Rio, Cuba 22 26N 83 40W
15 Pindos Oros, Greece 40 0N 21 0E
21 Piracicaba, Brazil 22 45S 47 30W
15 Piraeus = Piraiévs
15 Piraiévs, Greece 37 57N 23 42E
14 Pisa, Italy 43 43N 10 23E
14 Pistóia, Italy 43 57N 10 53E
16 Piteå, Sweden 65 55N 21 25E
8 Pitlochry, Scotland 56 43N 3 43W
37 Pittsburgh, U.S.A. 40 25N 79 55W
40 Piura, Peru 5 5S 80 45W
42 Plata, Rio de la, S. America 35 30S 56 0W
36 Platte, R., U.S.A. 41 0N 98 0W
10 Plauen, W. Germany 50 29N 12 9E
28 Plenty, B. of, N.Z. 37 45S 177 0E
11 Pleven, Bulgaria 43 26N 24 37E
11 Ploiești, Rumania 44 57N 26 5E
11 Plovdiv, Bulgaria 42 8N 24 44E
7 Plymouth, England 50 23N 4 9W
11 Plzen, Czechoslovakia 49 45N 13 22E
14 Po, R., Italy 45 0N 10 45E
39 Pointe-à-Pitre, Guadaloupe 16 10N 61 30W
39 Pointe-Noire, Congo 4 48S 12 0E
12 Poitiers, France 46 35N 0 20W
11 Poland, st., Europe 52 0N 20 0E
18 Poltava, U.S.S.R. 49 35N 34 35E
39 Ponce, Puerto Rico 18 0N 66 50W
42 Ponta Grossa, Brazil 25 0S 50 10W
12 Pontevedra, Spain 42 26N 8 40W
23 Pontianak, Indonesia 0 3S 109 15E
7 Poole, England 50 42N 2 2W
22 Poona, India 18 29N 73 57E
17 Pori, Finland 61 29N 21 48E
32 Port-au-Prince, Haiti 18 40N 72 20W
27 Port Augusta, Australia 32 30S 137 50E
27 Port Chalmers, N.Z. 45 49S 170 30E
33 Port Elizabeth, S. Africa 33 58S 25 40E
8 Port Glasgow, Scotland 55 57N 4 40W
30 Port Harcourt, Nigeria 4 40N 7 10E
26 Port Hedland, Australia 20 25S 118 35E
9 Port Laoise, Ireland 53 2N 7 20W
27 Port Lincoln, Australia 34 42S 135 52E
27 Port Macquarie, Australia 31 25S 152 54E
3 Port Moresby, Papua New Guinea 9 24S 147 8E
39 Port of Spain, Trinidad 10 40N 61 20W
27 Port Pirie, Australia 33 10S 137 58E
31 Port Said = Bûr Saîd 31 28N 32 6E
31 Port Sudan = Bûr Sûdân 31 28N 32 6E
7 Port Talbot, Wales 51 35N 3 48W
34 Portage la Prairie, Canada 49 58N 98 18W
13 Portland, U.S.A. 45 35N 122 40W
7 Portland Bill, Pt., England 50 31N 2 27W
13 Pôrto, Portugal 41 8N 8 40W
42 Pôrto Alegre, Brazil 30 5S 51 3W
8 Portree, Scotland 57 25N 6 11W
37 Portsmouth, U.S.A. 36 50N 76 20W
7 Portsmouth, England 50 48N 1 6W
13 Portugal, Rep., Europe 40 0N 7 0W
42 Posadas, Spain 37 47N 5 11W
40 Potosi, Bolivia 19 38S 65 50W
10 Potsdam, Germany 52 23N 13 4E
7 Powys, Co., Wales 53 30N 3 30W
10 Poznan, Poland 52 25N 17 0E
11 Praha (Prague) Cz. 50 5N 14 22E
14 Prato, Italy 43 53N 11 5E
6 Preston, England 53 46N 2 42W
8 Prestwick, Scotland 55 30N 4 38W
33 Pretoria, S. Africa 25 44S 28 12E
34 Prince Albert, Canada 53 15N 105 50W
35 Prince Edward I., Canada 46 20N 63 0W
34 Prince Georoe, Canada 53 50N 122 50W
34 Prince Rupert, Canada 54 20N 130 20W
18 Prokopyevsk, 54 0N 87 3E
22 Prome, Burma 18 45N 95 30E
39 Providence, U.S.A. 41 41N 71 15W
34 Prudhoe Bay, Australia 21 30S 149 30W
18 Pskov, U.S.S.R. 57 50N 28 25E
38 Puebla, Mexico 19 0N 98 10W
36 Pueblo, U.S.A. 38 20N 104 40W
39 Puerto Montt, Chile 41 28S 73 0W
39 Puerto Plata, Dominican Rep. 19 40N 70 45W
39 Puerto Rico I., W. Indies 18 10N 66 30W
14 Pula, Yugoslavia 44 54N 13 57E
22 Punakha, Bhutan 27 42N 89 52E
42 Punta Arenas, Chile 53 0S 71 0W
39 Puntarenas, Costa Rica 10 0N 84 50W
42 Purus, R., Brazil 5 25S 64 0W
25 Pusan, S. Korea 35 5N 129 0E
25 Pyongyang, N. Korea 39 0N 125 30E
13 Pyrénées, Mts., Europe 42 45N 1 0E

Q
21 Qatar, st., Asia 25 30N 51 15E
31 Qena, Egypt 26 10N 32 43E
35 Quebec, Canada 46 52N 71 13W
34 Queen Charlotte I., Canada 53 10N 132 0W
2 Queen Elizabeth Is., Canada 75 0N 95 0W
33 Quelimane, Mozambique 17 53S 36 58E
38 Querétaro, Mexico 20 40N 100 23W
22 Quetta, Pakistan 30 15N 66 55E
23 Quezon City, Phil. 14 50N 121 0E
12 Quimper, France 48 0N 4 9W
40 Quito, Ecuador 0 15S 78 35W

R
30 Rabat, Morocco 33 9N 6 53W
3 Rabaul, Papua New Guinea 4 24S 152 18E
14 Ragusa, Italy 36 56N 14 42E
22 Rajkot, India 22 15N 70 56E

37 Raleigh, U.S.A. 35 46N 78 38W
17 Randers, Denmark 56 29N 10 1E
22 Rangoon, Burma 16 45N 96 20E
28 Rarotonga, I., Pacific Oc. 21 30S 160 0W
21 Rasht, Iran 37 20N 49 40E
5 Rathlin, I., N. Ireland 55 18N 6 14W
17 Rauma, Finland 61 10N 21 30E
14 Ravenna, Italy 44 28N 12 15E
14 Rawalpindi, Pakistan 33 38N 73 8E
41 Recife, Brazil 8 0S 35 0W
34 Red Deer, Canada 52 20N 113 50W
21 Red Sea, Africa/Asia 25 0N 36 0E
10 Regensburg, W. Germany 49 1N 12 7E
14 Réggio, Italy 38 7N 15 38E
34 Regina, Canada 50 30N 104 35W
12 Reims, France 49 15N 4 0E
34 Reindeer L., Canada 57 20N 102 20W
34 Renfrew, Scotland 55 52N 4 24W
12 Rennes, France 48 7N 1 41W
36 Reno, U.S.A. 39 30N 119 50W
42 Resistencia, Argentina 27 30N 59 0W
32 Réunion, I., Indian Oc. 22 0S 56 0E
34 Revelstoke, Canada 51 0N 118 0W
15 Reykjavik, Iceland 64 10N 22 0W
15 Rhodes = Ródhos, I.
12 Rhine, R., W. Germany 51 42N 6 20E
7 Rhondda, Wales 51 40N 3 30W
12 Rhône, R., France 43 28N 4 42E
8 Rhum, I., Scotland 57 0N 6 20W
41 Ribeirno Prêto, Brazil 21 10S 47 50W
28 Riccarton, N.Z. 43 32S 172 37E
37 Richland, U.S.A. 46 15N 119 15W
37 Richmond, U.S.A. 37 33N 77 27W
18 Riga, U.S.S.R. 56 58N 24 12E
14 Rijeka, Yugoslavia 45 20N 14 21E
14 Rímini, Italy 44 3N 12 33E
35 Rimouski, Canada 48 27N 68 30W
41 Rio de Janeiro, Brazil 22 50S 43 0W
42 Rio Gallegos, Arg. 51 45S 69 20W
41 Rio Grande, Brazil 32 0S 52 20W
36 Rio Grande, R., U.S.A. 35 45N 106 20W
35 Rivière du Loup, Canada 47 50N 69 30W
21 Riyadh, see Ar Riyad 24 40N 46 50E
37 Roanoke, U.S.A. 37 19N 79 55W
12 Rochdale, England 53 36N 2 10W
12 Rochefort, France 45 56N 0 57W
37 Rochester, U.S.A. 43 10N 77 40W
37 Rockford, U.S.A. 42 20N 89 0W
27 Rockhampton, Australia 23 22S 150 32E
14 Ródhos, I., Greece 36 15N 28 10E
14 Roma, Australia 26 32S 148 49E
14 Roma, (Rome) Italy 41 54N 12 30E
42 Rosario, Argentina 33 0S 60 40W
9 Roscommon & Co., Ireland 53 38N 8 11W
17 Roskilde, Denmark 55 38N 12 3E
3 Ross Dependency, Antarctica 70 0S 170 5W
3 Ross Sea, Antarctica 74 0S 178 0E
9 Rosslare, Ireland 52 17N 6 23W
16 Rostock, E. Germany 54 4N 12 9E
18 Rostov, U.S.S.R. 47 15N 39 45E
8 Rosyth, Scotland 56 2N 3 26W
6 Rotherham, England 53 26N 1 21W
10 Rothesay, Scotland 55 50N 5 3W
28 Rotorua, N.Z. 38 9S 176 16E
10 Rotterdam, Neth. 51 55N 4 30E
12 Roubaix, France 50 40N 3 10E
12 Rouen, France 49 27N 1 4E
35 Rouyn, Canada 48 20N 79 0W
17 Rovaniemi, Finland 66 29N 25 41E
18 Rovno, U.S.S.R. 50 40N 26 10E
21 Rub'al Khali, desert, Saudi Arabia 21 0N 51 0E
18 Rubtsovsk, U.S.S.R. 51 30N 80 50E
11 Rumania, st. Europe 46 0N 25 0E
18 Ruse, Bulgaria 43 48N 25 59E
8 Rugby, England 52 23N 1 16W
11 Rutherglen, Scotland 55 50N 4 11W
30 Rwanda, st., Africa 2 30S 30 0E
18 Ryazan, U.S.S.R. 54 40N 39 40E
18 Rybinsk, U.S.S.R. 58 5N 38 50E

S
10 Saarbrücken, W. Germany 49 15N 6 58E
13 Sabadell, Spain 41 28N 2 7E
23 Sabah, Malaysia 6 0N 117 0E
36 Sacramento, U.S.A. 38 39N 121 30E
37 Saginaw, U.S.A. 43 26N 83 55W
30 Sahara, desert, Africa 23 0N 5 0W
23 Saigon, see Phan Bho Ho Chi Minh, Vietnam 10 58N 106 40E
37 St. Albans, England 51 44N 0 19W
8 St. Andrews, Scotland 56 20N 2 48W
7 St. Austell, England 50 20N 4 48W
34 St. Boniface, Canada 49 50N 97 10W
39 St. Christopher', I., W. Indies 17 20N 62 40W
7 St. David's Hd., Wales 51 54N 5 16W
12 St. Etienne, France 45 27N 4 22E
5 St. George's Chan., Br. Isles 52 0N 6 0W
29 St. Helena, I., Atlantic Oc. 15 55S 5 44W
6 St. Helens, England 53 28N 2 44W
35 St. Hyacinthe, Canada 45 40N 72 58W
29 Saint John, Canada 45 20N 66 8W
35 St. John's, Canada 47 33N 52 40W
37 St. Joseph, U.S.A. 39 40N 94 50W
8 St. Kilda, I., Scotland 57 9N 8 34W
35 St. Lawrence, G. of, Canada 48 25N 62 0W
35 St. Lawrence, R., Canada 49 30N 66 0W
30 St. Louis, Senegal 16 8N 16 27W
37 St. Louis, U.S.A. 38 40N 90 20W
39 St. Lucia, I., Windward Is., 14 0N 60 50W
12 St. Malo, France 48 40 2 0W

12 St. Nazaire, France 47 18N 2 11W
37 St. Paul, U.S.A. 44 54N 93 5W
37 St. Petersburg, U.S.A. 27 45N 82 40W
35 St. Pierre and Miquelon, N. America 46 49N 56 15W
12 St. Quentin, France 49 55N 3 20E
39 St. Vincent, I., Windward Is., 13 10N 61 10W
24 Sakai, Japan 34 35N 135 27E
19 Sakhalin, I., U.S.S.R. 51 0N 143 0E
42 Salado, R., Argentina 35 40S 58 10W
12 Salamanca, Spain 40 57N 5 40W
22 Salem, India 11 39N 78 12E
14 Salerno, Italy 40 40N 14 44E
7 Salisbury, England 51 4N 1 48W
33 Salisbury, Rhodesia 17 50N 31 2E
7 Salisbury Plain, England 51 13N 2 0W
41 Salvador, Brazil 13 0S 38 30W
38 Salvador, st., Central America 13 50N 89 0W
36 Salt Lake City, U.S.A. 40 45N 112 0W
42 Salta, Argentina 24 48S 65 30W
38 Saltillo, Mexico 25 30N 100 57W
10 Salzburg, Austria 47 48N 13 2E
23 Samar, I., Philippines 12 0N 125 0E
18 Samarkand, U.S.S.R. 39 40N 67 0E
21 Samsun, Turkey 41 15N 36 15E
36 San Angelo, U.S.A. 31 30N 100 30W
42 San Cristóbal, Ven. 7 35N 72 24W
36 San Diego, U.S.A. 32 50N 117 10W
39 San Fernando, Trinidad 37 45N 122 30W
36 San Francisco, U.S.A. 37 45N 122 30W
39 San Francisco de Macoris, Dominican Rep. 19 19N 70 15W
39 San José, Costa Rica 10 0N 84 2W
42 San Juan, Argentina 31 30S 68 30W
38 San Luis Potosí, Mex. 22 10N 101 0W
14 San Marino, Italy 43 56N 12 25E
42 San Miguel de Tucumán, Argentina 26 47S 65 13W
38 San Pedro de las Colonias, Mexico 25 50N 102 59W
42 San Salvador, Salvador 13 40N 89 20W
13 San Sebastian, Spain 43 17N 1 58W
21 San'a, Yemen 15 27N 44 12E
17 Sandviken, Sweden 60 38N 16 46E
38 Santa Ana, Salvador 14 0N 89 40W
42 Santa Ana, U.S.A. 33 48N 117 55W
36 Santa Barbara, U.S.A. 34 25N 119 40W
36 Santa Barbara Is., U.S.A. 33 40N 119 40W
42 Santa Clara, Cuba 22 20N 80 0W
30 Santa Cruz, Tenerife 28 29N 16 26W
42 Santa Fé, Argentina 31 35S 60 41W
40 Santa Marta, Colombia 11 15N 74 13W
13 Santander, Spain 43 27N 3 51W
41 Santarém, Brazil 2 25S 54 42W
13 Santarém, Portugal 39 12N 8 42W
39 Santiago, Chile 33 24S 70 50W
13 Santiago, Spain 42 52N 8 37W
42 Santiago de Cuba, Cuba 20 0N 75 49W
42 Santiago del Estero, Argentina 27 50S 64 20W
39 Santo Domingo, Dominican Rep. 18 30N 69 58W
41 Santos, Brazil 24 0S 46 20W
41 São Carlos, Brazil 22 0S 47 50W
42 São Luis, Brazil 2 39S 44 15W
41 São Marcos, B. de, Brazil 2 0S 44 0W
41 São Paulo, Brazil 23 40S 46 50W
41 São Roque, C. de, Brazil 5 30S 35 10W
12 Saône, R., France 46 25N 4 50E
24 Sapporo, Japan 43 0N 141 15E
15 Sarajevo, Yugoslavia 43 52N 18 26E
18 Saransk, U.S.S.R. 54 10N 45 10E
18 Saratov, U.S.S.R. 51 30N 46 2E
23 Sarawak, Malaysia 2 0N 113 0E
14 Sardinia, I., Italy 40 0N 9 0E
17 Sarpsborg, Norway 59 16N 11 12E
18 Sasebo, Japan 33 15N 129 50E
34 Saskatoon, Canada 52 10N 106 45W
14 Sássari, Italy 40 44N 8 33E
21 Saudi Arabia, st., Asia 26 0N 44 0E
35 Saulte Ste. Marie, Canada 46 30N 84 20W
17 Sava, R., Yugoslavia 44 40N 19 50E
37 Savannah, U.S.A. 32 4N 81 4W
14 Savona, Italy 44 19N 8 29E
7 Sca Fell, Mt., England 54 27N 3 14W
6 Scarborough, England 54 17N 0 24W
9 Scilly, Is., England 49 55N 6 15W
8 Scotland, U.K. 57 0N 4 0W
37 Scranton, U.S.A. 41 22N 75 41W
6 Scunthorpe, England 53 35N 0 38W
35 Seattle, U.S.A. 47 36N 122 20W
12 Seine, R., France 49 28N 0 15E
18 Semipalatinsk, U.S.S.R. 50 30N 80 10E
24 Sendai, Japan 31 50N 130 20E
30 Senegal, R., Senegal 16 30N 15 30W
30 Senegal, st., W. Africa 14 30N 14 30W
30 Sept Îles, Canada 50 8N 66 22W
18 Serov, U.S.S.R. 59 40N 60 20E
33 Serowe, Botswana 22 18S 26 58E
12 Sète, France 43 25N 3 42E
13 Setúbal, Portugal 38 30N 8 58W
18 Sevastopol, U.S.S.R. 44 35N 33 30E
6 Severn, R., U.K. 52 15N 2 13W
18 Severodinsk, U.S.S.R. 64 27N 39 58E
13 Sevilla, Spain 37 23N 6 0W
34 Seward, Alaska 60 0N 149 30W
20 Seychelles, Is., Indian Oc. 5 0S 56 0E
31 Sfax, Tunisia 34 49N 10 48E
10 s'Gravenhage, Neth. 52 7N 4 17E
18 Shakhty, U.S.S.R. 47 0N 40 10E
25 Shanghai, China 31 15N 121 30E
9 Shannon, R., Ireland 53 10N 8 10W
25 Shantow, China 23 25N 116 40E
6 Sheffield, England 53 23N 1 28W
27 Shellharbour, Australia 34 31S 150 51E